family field guide
— S E R I E S —

VOLUME FIVE

The Night Sky

STARS . CONSTELLATIONS . STORIES

written by
Garrick Pfaffmann

BearBop Press LLC

BASALT COLORADO USA

family field guide

— S E R I E S —

field notes

family field guide
— SERIES —

field notes

ISBN

978-1-936905-96-6

Copyright 2011 by Garrick Pfaffmann.

All rights reserved.

PUBLISHED BY

BearBop Press, LLC

www.bearboppress.com

bearboppress@yahoo.com

ILLUSTRATED BY

Aspen Community School students

Woody Creek, Colorado

BOOK DESIGN

words pictures colours graphic design

Basalt, Colorado

DISTRIBUTED BY

People's Press

Globe Piquot Press

LIBRARY OF CONGRESS CONTROL NUMBER

2011925592

Author's Dedication

To those who enjoy looking...and seeing
In daytime....and night.
So much splendor is out there waiting to be admired,
And so many questions are waiting to be asked.

Acknowledgements

Thanks to the many people who carefully helped to shape this book and especially to the students of Aspen Community School for sharing the constellations, the stories and their artwork. Special thanks to Lindsay, Mason and Bo for their patience and ideas, to Anne W. Siewert and Rebekkah Davis for their careful editing, Kelly Alford for the brilliant design work and publishing expertise, and to Mirte Mallory for sending us on our trajectory to the stars. You all are proof that we most certainly can accomplish more as a whole than any individual by ourselves.

Other Titles in the Family Field Guide Series

Introduction

Most of my life, I have had only slight interest in stars. I have looked up on starry nights and been blown away by the band of stars that is the Milky Way, but I've mostly viewed the night sky as a huge mass of darkness with tiny spots of light in its midst.

It appears that I am not alone. Only in the past few generations has stargazing been isolated to a relatively small number of hobbyists and highly trained astronomers. In contrast, for tens of thousands of years, understanding the stars was a way of life for all of humankind throughout the world. Before electricity, compasses and calendars, the stars were the primary tool for storytelling, navigation and the measurement of time. In a world of insecurity and unpredictability, the stars, the moon and the sun were the only constants in life. While sitting around the fire at night, humans noticed the stars. They recognized and recorded the consistent patterns in their movements, making astronomy one of the oldest of all sciences.

My initial interest in the stars stemmed from wanting to recognize some of these patterns better. I wanted to see if I could match the seasons with the rising of specific constellations and to see if I could predict where the sun would rise and set throughout the year. This lead to further reading...and further understanding that there is a LOT of very cool stuff out there.

As more time is invested in observation, more interesting observations occur. What I thought was barren blackness with a million spots of white light is actually vast space filled with new stars being born, rocks the size of continents whizzing through the darkness, bright and contrasting colors, and a dynamic system that is ever-changing and interesting to observe. With access to only a pair of binoculars or a small telescope, much of the beauty in the sky lies beyond physical appearance; the magic requires an understanding of what you are seeing. It is helpful to know that a dusty cloud of light contains several billion stars that lie several thousand light years away; that a particular star in the sky is nearly as large as half of our solar system; that the light leaving certain stars has been traveling through space since the time of King Tut and is only now reaching our eyes.

Gaining a foothold of interest   sky requires an understanding of the patterns and glimmers of light that are the stars. Though subtle, the night sky holds wonders beyond our understanding. In the same way that a field guide helps to make the birds, plants, mammals and bugs of our own biosphere more interesting and enjoyable, the same tool is even more helpful when interpreting the night sky. I hope that this guide is the beginning of many observations and new journeys!

How To Use This Book

The following features are included in this book to help beginning sky watchers navigate the night sky and to provide a brief introduction to astronomy.

When and Where On the left side of each page is a list of the months when each *constellation* is in view, when it is overhead and a quick reference for how to find it. The months and overhead schedules are based on the constellations' locations one hour after sunset from the viewpoint at 40 degrees north latitude, the mid-latitude for the United States. Use these dates and locations in conjunction with the star maps in the back of the book.

Fun Observations The "fun observations" in the sky have nothing to do with the constellations themselves; the constellation is simply a reference point to finding galaxies, star clusters, nebulae, supernovas and more. Most of these objects are visible with binoculars unless otherwise noted, and they allow practice for more precise sky hunting. The locations of these features are indicated on each Constellation Map.

Historical Notes Historical notes are provided as a brief history of astronomy from varying cultures and notable historical discoveries. These paint a picture of the long and widespread history of astronomy dating back thousands of years on all continents.

Constellation Map The constellation maps show the main stars in each constellation, the connect-the-dot pattern of the stars and includes the names of the brightest stars and their distances. Usually, the brightest star in the constellation is known as the Alpha star, the second brightest is known as the Beta star, but that is not always the case. The distances of the stars demonstrate the vast depth in space; a difference of 1 light year between stars means that they are separated by 6 trillion miles (see p. 14). Notice the vast depth between the stars within a single constellation!

Urania's Mirror Many of the constellations include an image of the stars recorded in 1825 in a series of pictures titled Urania's Mirror. These old star charts depict the stars and their representative characters.

Star Maps Four Star Maps are located in the back of the book, one map per season. They are based on observations from 40 degrees north latitude. People living north of 40 degrees will see more of the northern horizon and less of the southern, so the overhead portion of the map will shift slightly north. Those living south of 40 degrees will see more of the southern horizon and the overhead point will shift slightly south. These maps describe the sky one hour past sunset within the given month. Note that the cardinal directions on the map are messed up! The maps are intended to be held overhead in front of your eyes as you are looking upwards at the sky. This is a much easier way to observe the map AND the stars, rather than holding the book down on the ground, then lifting your head and looking upwards while trying to remember the map description.

Contents

Star-Watching Tips

With a little practice, stargazing can shift from casually staring at a dark sky to a useful and enjoyable naturalist skill. Following are a few helpful tips to make your star-watching experiences more rewarding.

Dark Skies A good view of the stars requires a dark sky. While the full moon is fun to see, its light dims the stars dramatically, so best try to pick a moonless night to find the constellations. It is also helpful to find a dark, treeless, wide horizon away from town lights to see more subtle features. Even a single street light will dim the stars dramatically.

Night Vision The longer you are out in the night, the more accustomed your eyes become to seeing dimmer light. After 20 minutes in the night, your eyes are best adapted to picking up the dimmest light in the sky. Avoid using headlamps or flashlights so your eyes can see to their best potential. If you need to look at a star map while out at night, cover your flashlight with red cellophane or use a red bulb; this will allow you to read without killing your night vision.

Binoculars Telescopes are the obvious tool for observing stars, but binoculars are the simplest tool and a good pair will reveal hidden wonders with ease. Don't become fixated on using a telescope; for beginning sky watchers, the telescope can become the focus of the experience rather than the stars themselves.

Look Small Pick a region of the sky, focus on that area and see what you can find. Looking around the entire sky in one glance can become disorienting and you'll find yourself spinning in circles. I like to start in the eastern sky to see the constellations that are just rising (it's easier on the neck), then look to the western sky to see what is just setting (also easy on the neck), then to the south, then to the north, and finally, straight overhead.

Field Guides and Star Maps A guide to the night sky is helpful when learning to navigate the stars. Read your books and maps before going out so that you have an idea about where to look and what to see. Bring books with you to help navigate for new unseen features.

Stay Warm! Be prepared for cold weather. It's always disappointing to go through the effort of getting outside at night, only to leave early due to chilly fingers, toes and ears. So take warm clothes if there is a chance that the weather might get cold.

Lawn Chairs Stargazing requires looking up which can result in a kinked neck after just a few minutes. A reclining lawn chair can help you look up without tweaking your neck. Lying flat on a blanket works, but can reveal so much of the sky that it becomes disorienting.

Friends and Family Sharing an experience with friends and family makes for more memorable and enjoyable exploring. Friends and family members can share their knowledge, stories, vision and laughter, and make the experience more fun.

Constellations

Constellations are human-made ideas. People have looked up at the stars for thousands of years and have connected the stars in meaningful ways to help create some familiarity out of the millions of lights overhead. In some cases, like Orion, the Big Dipper and Cygnus the Swan, the constellation drawings created thousands of years ago actually look something like what they are supposed to represent. In other cases, however, the images created in mythology require a huge stretch of the imagination. In these situations, I like to imagine my own drawings among these stars and see what other creatures my mind can create.

Stars in the sky can seem random and without order....

Once they are connected, in your imagination, they take on a bit of meaning...

When used to create an image, they take on more meaning.
Constellations were designed to bring meaning to the sky.

A Reference Point Constellations work together to create a map of the sky. This map provides a reference point when looking for particular objects in the sky. Familiarize yourself with the "night-time guidepost" constellations (p. 16-17) and use these easy-to-find star-pictures to help navigate the sky. As in all things, find something that is familiar to get your bearings, then use these reference points for easy navigation of harder-to-find features.

Story Telling The early civilizations who created the constellations used the stars as a basis for sharing stories. Great leaders, hunters, musicians, animals and events are recorded in the stars. The star pictures have allowed stories to be passed down through generations. Many separate groups of people from diverse cultures have shared stories of bulls, scorpions, lions and bears using the same exact sets of stars (Taurus, Scorpio, Leo and Ursa Major). As in the game "telephone," most of the stories have changed over several thousand years, but the constellations have remained constant and still inspire bedtime stories.

family field guide

The Night Sky

Recognizing that the sky is much more than an empty flat screen with countless white spots is the starting point for meaningful stargazing. While the stars look as if they are side by side, they are not. Stars are in front of each other and behind each other and the amount of space between them, even between those that appear close together, is enormous. The next important realization about the night sky is that it is active. Even in the dark spaces, there are rocks flying around, stars getting ready to explode, stars being born, enormous clouds of billowing gas, stars that are orbiting each other and all sorts of activity. The challenge with seeing this movement is that it is all happening so far away. For now, it is good enough to realize that the night sky, like a forest, is a dynamic place with lots of activity; it is all just happening very far away.

This photograph taken in 1990 from over 3 billion miles into space highlights Earth, a "pale blue dot" in the vastness of space, as noted by Carl Sagan in his book The Cosmos. *The night sky is not flat; there is space unimaginable between all of the dots in the night sky.*

What Is A Star?

A star, in its simplest explanation, is a mass of fiery Hydrogen gas. Our sun is a star, just like any other; it just happens to be close enough to earth that its heat and light provides us with daylight and warmth. Out there in the darkness of space, Hydrogen gas is the most common element, and Helium gas, the stuff that makes balloons fly, is the second most common element. Certain activities happen in space that make Hydrogen and Helium gases pool together in tight little clouds (called *nebulae*). As a gas cloud gathers tighter and tighter, the Hydrogen molecules join together, or fuse. This process is called *nuclear fusion*. When this happens, huge amounts of energy and light are released and the fiery furnace that we call a star is born. Once the fire starts, the Hydrogen gas keeps burning until it runs out. The formation of new stars may take hundreds of millions of years and, once formed, the star will continue to burn anywhere between several hundred million years for large stars, to several trillion years for smaller stars.

How Bright Are The Stars?

Apparent Magnitude As we look up in the sky, some stars are very bright while others are quite dim. Scientists long ago came up with a scale to describe the brightness of stars called the *apparent magnitude scale*. Bright stars are given a low magnitude number, while dim stars are given a higher number. The scale seems backwards. I would give bright stars bigger numbers, but this ancient measuring scale has lasted over 2,000 years, so why change it now? The brightest planet in the sky, Venus, has a magnitude of -4.5, while bright stars have magnitudes of 0-1. People can see stars and other objects up to magnitude 4.5 with the naked eye, up to magnitude 6.5 with binoculars and up to magnitude 8.5 with a small telescope.

Absolute Magnitude While the apparent magnitude describes how brightly we see the stars, it explains nothing about how much light a star produces. A star that emits very little light and is close to earth can look very bright, while a very bright star that is much farther away will look dim. Scientists use a different scale, called *absolute magnitude,* to describe how much light a star emits. This scale measures the brightness of stars as if they were all an equal distance from Earth. The table below compares the absolute and apparent magnitudes of the ten brightest stars in the Northen Hemisphere sky.

Star Name	Constellation	Apparent Magnitude	Absolute Magnitude	Distance (light years)
Sirius	Canis Major	-1.46	1.42	8.6
Arcturus	Bootes	-0.04	-0.29	36.7
Vega	Lyra	0.03	0.58	25.3
Capella	Auriga	0.08	0.58	42.2
Rigel	Orion	0.12	0.35	777
Procyon	Canis Minor	0.38	2.65	11.4
Betelgeuse	Orion	0.5	-6.05	429
Altair	Aquila	0.77	2.21	16.8
Aldebaran	Taurus	0.85	-0.63	65
Antares	Scorpius	0.96	-5.28	604

Sirius is the brightest star in the sky with an apparent magnitude of -1.46, but Betelgeuse puts out the most light of these stars with an absolute magnitude of -6.05

family field guide

Why Do Stars Move?

If you look at the sky throughout the night you will notice that the stars appear to move. Like the sun and the moon, they rise in the east, move across the sky throughout the night, then set in the west. However, as with the sun, the stars are not moving. Instead, it is Earth's movement through space that causes the changing nighttime scenery.

The earth's spinning motion around its axis (*rotation*) causes the stars to move across the sky throughout the night and the earth's movement around the sun (*revolution* or *orbit*) causes different stars and constellations to come into view throughout the year.

First, the earth is constantly spinning around its axis. It completes a full rotation every 24 hours. This creates the 24-hour day/night cycle. As the earth spins, the stars rise in the east and they climb higher in the sky before setting below the western horizon. The North Star is located directly above the earth's northern axis point, so even while the earth is spinning, that one star does not change position. All of the other stars appear to rotate around the North Star because of Earth's spinning rotation.

While the earth is spinning on its axis, it is also *revolving*, or *orbiting*, around the sun. The earth revolves around the sun every 365^{1}/$_{4}$ days. This is the length of one year. This larger movement through space means that we pass by different stars as we travel around the sun, giving us the changing view of the sky throughout the year.

Knowing how the stars move each night and how the constellations change throughout the year has allowed civilizations to predict the seasons and create calendars for thousands of years.

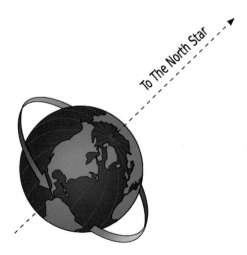

Earth's rotation causes stars to rise and set each night, except for the North Star which remains stationary.

Earth's orbit around the sun causes constellations to change throughout the seasons.

How Big Are Stars?

While all stars look relatively similar from where we stand here on Earth, their sizes vary to the extreme. Our sun is an average-sized star, though it is 100 times larger than Earth. Many stars are smaller than our sun, but even the smallest star (Wolf 359) is much larger than any of the planets in our solar system. At the other end of the spectrum are the very large stars, called *red giants*, which are much, much larger than our sun. Deneb, the brightest star in the constellation Cygnus, is approximately 200 times larger than our sun and 2,000 times the size of Earth. If it were located in the same place as our sun, it would engulf the first four planets and would just barely touch Jupiter! The pictures at right compare the sizes of Earth, other planets and other stars within the Milky Way galaxy.

How Far Away?

Stars are really, really far away. They are so far away that it is almost impossible to really understand the distances. In our daily lives, we may walk a few miles, a long drive may cover a few hundred miles, a plane trip across the United States covers about 3,000 miles and a flight overseas might cover 5,000 miles or more. These are the distances that we use in our earthly travels.

In comparison, the distance from the earth to the moon is nearly 239,000 miles, the equivalent of 25 round trip visits between Denver and London. The sun is much, much farther away at 93 million miles. The distances from the sun and the moon are huge, but they are a walk in the park compared to the distances used to describe the stars.

Stars are so far away that astronomers begin to measure their distances in *light years* (ly) instead of miles. Light is the fastest moving thing in the universe, traveling over 186,000 miles per second. The light reflected off the moon takes a bit more than one second to travel to Earth and light from the sun takes about 8.5 minutes to travel to Earth. But stars are so far away, light takes years, sometimes many, many years, to travel to Earth. In one year, light travels nearly **6 trillion** miles.

The closest star to our solar system is called Alpha Centauri and is over 4 light years away, more than 24 trillion miles! If a person were to count really, really fast, like 3 numbers per second, it would take over 260,000 years to count to 24 trillion! And that is the closest star to Earth outside of our solar system! By comparison, one visible star called Erakis is over 5,000 light years distant! By definition, the light that we see today left that star 5,000 years ago, 2,000 years before King Tut ruled Egypt.

To show the distance between our sun and the next closest star, Alpha Centauri, imagine that our sun is the size of a grapefruit. By comparison, Earth is the tip of a ballpoint pen. Earth, the pen tip, is located in Los Angeles. The sun, in this size comparison, is located half a football field away. Alpha Centauri would be located in New York City! There is a lot of space between the stars!

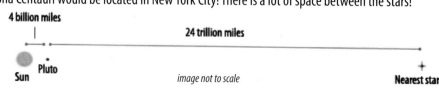

4 billion miles

24 trillion miles

Sun Pluto *image not to scale* Nearest star

family field guide

(1)

Mercury · Mars · Venus · Earth

Earth is the largest of the *inner planets*, the four closest planets to the sun.

(2)

Earth · Neptune · Uranus · Saturn · Jupiter

Earth is tiny compared to the *outer planets*, those beyond Earth's orbit.

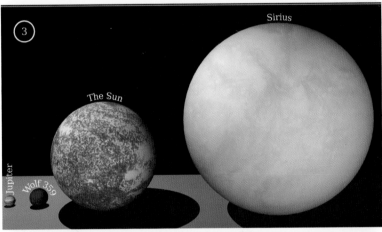

(3)

Jupiter · Wolf 359 · The Sun · Sirius

Even the smallest star, Wolf 359, is larger than Jupiter, the biggest planet in our solar system. Our sun is much smaller than the brightest star in the sky, Sirius.

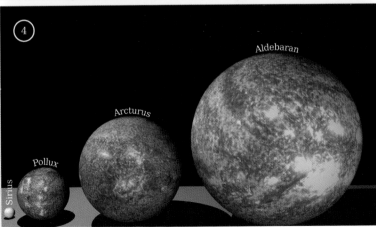

(4)

Sirius · Pollux · Arcturus · Aldebaran

Some stars are so big, they make our own sun look like a small dot in the universe.

family field guide

Nighttime Guideposts

Many constellations are difficult to find for beginning sky watchers. Using easy-to-find constellations as guideposts makes it possible to find the hard-to-find star-pictures. Knowing these four constellations helps locate nearly twenty others nearby.

Cassiopeia Leads to Perseus the hero (fall and winter), Pegasus the flying horse (fall and winter) and Cepheus the king (year round).

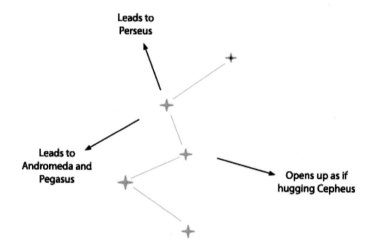

The Big Dipper Leads to Ursa Minor (year round), Leo the lion (in winter and spring) and Bootes the farmer (in summer and fall).

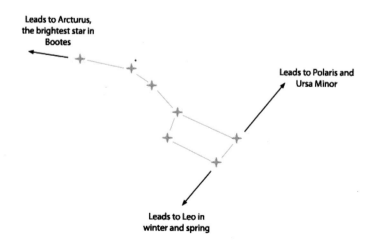

Winter Guidepost

Orion This is the brightest constellation in the winter sky and is the guidepost to five nearby star figures, all with obvious bright stars of their own.

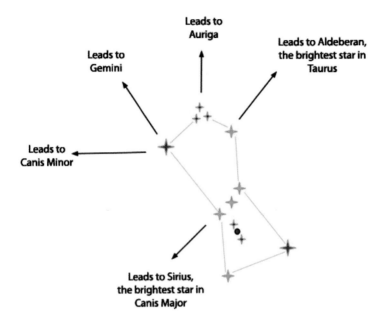

Leads to Auriga

Leads to Gemini

Leads to Aldeberan, the brightest star in Taurus

Leads to Canis Minor

Leads to Sirius, the brightest star in Canis Major

Summer Guidepost

Summer Triangle Three of the brightest stars in the summer and autumn sky are arranged in a huge triangle. They are not a constellation themselves, but are a guide to six others nearby.

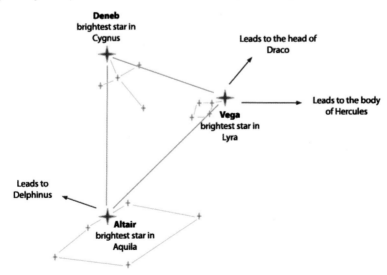

Deneb brightest star in Cygnus

Leads to the head of Draco

Leads to the body of Hercules

Vega brightest star in Lyra

Leads to Delphinus

Altair brightest star in Aquila

family field guide

Aquila
The Eagle

MONTHS IN THE SKY
June-December

OVERHEAD
September

BRIGHTEST STAR
Altair (magnitude 0.8)

FIND IT
On summer and fall nights, locate the three brightest stars in the sky which form the Summer Triangle. The southern-most of these stars is Altair, the brightest star in Aquila. Two stars line up on either side of Altair to form a nearly-straight line. Using these three stars, look for the broad diamond shape which forms the eagle's wings.

FUN OBSERVATIONS
M11 DUCK CLUSTER
This open cluster is barely visible through binoculars, but is more interesting with a small telescope.
Magnitude 7.0

HISTORICAL NOTES
Ancient China (4,000 BC-present)
China had an advanced civilization dating back well before that of ancient Egypt, and, as in many ancient civilizations, astronomy was a major part of their scientific observation. Records of a lunar eclipse have been discovered dating back to 1311 BC. Several observatories were in use by 700 BC and were used for 1,500 years, probably for the purpose of determining the ancient Chinese calendar. By 350 BC, they had developed a calendar based on the 365 1/4 days of the solar year.

THE EVIL PET In the Greek myths, Aquila is Zeus' favorite pet, a wild eagle tamed by the god of the sky and the leader of the gods. Aquila was a wild eagle when Zeus first noticed him soaring over Mount Olympus. After a few sightings, Zeus started putting meat out on the gate to entice the bird closer. Like a falconer working with a wild bird, Zeus trained the eagle and they began to work together. In some ways, their relationship was like that between a mob boss and his hit man, with Aquila carrying out Zeus' dirty work. The best known of Aquila's jobs fell upon the god Prometheus. Prometheus was the one god who trusted humans. He wanted to allow the human race to become independent, to thrive and to make their own decisions free of the gods. Towards that end, Prometheus gave mankind the gift of fire. Zeus did not approve of this gift, nor of mankind's move towards freedom. As a way of punishing Prometheus for his poor judgement, Zeus chained him to a rock and sent the trusted eagle to eat away at Prometheus' liver. Being immortal, his belly healed each night such that he could never die. Just as he gained back his health each day, Zeus sent Aquila to peck away at him again. This torture went on for many years. In honor of the eagle's faithfulness, though gruesome and violent as it was, Zeus honored Aquila in the summer and fall sky, when the eagle flies most freely.

family field guide

Constellation Map

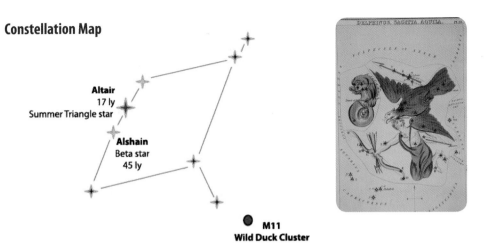

Altair
17 ly
Summer Triangle star

Alshain
Beta star
45 ly

M11
Wild Duck Cluster

Lacey Newhard
6th grade

NAME
Aquila is the Latin word meaning eagle.

EAGLE OR VULTURE
The eagle's wing span is viewed as the diamond shape and the tail is the line extending outward, as seen in the Constellation Map. With no head at all, it appears more like a vulture, and, in fact, the Romans viewed it as such. They called this constellaiton *Vultur volans*, the Flying Vulture. As is the way of constellations, use your imagination and see what looks best to you.

Aries
The Ram

MONTHS IN THE SKY
September-March

OVERHEAD
December

BRIGHTEST STAR
Hamal (magnitude 2.0)

FIND IT
Aries is tough to find as it has only three nondescript stars. First, find Cassiopeia, the big W. Follow the points of the W to the Great Square of Pegasus in the fall and winter sky. The three stars of Aries are quite alone in a dark part of the sky just east of the Great Square. It lies just below the Milky Way.

FUN OBSERVATIONS
MESARTHIM
The dimmest of Aries' three stars is actually a double star, but requires a small telescope to see the distinction. These two stars that appear so close together are actually 36 billion miles apart. By comparison, our sun is 93 million miles away from earth.
Magnitude 3.9

HISTORICAL NOTES
Babylon (2500 BC-200 BC)
In ancient times, the land in modern day Iraq was called Babylon. Astronomy there dates back to at least 1800 BC. These ancient star gazers understood the solar system in their efforts to create a calendar by which they could plan their daily lives. By 600 BC they had recorded movements of the stars, moon, sun and planets with great precision.

GENTLE HERO While most of the Greek myths involve lying, stealing, cheating and death, Aries the ram is placed in the stars for his community service work. His story can be appreciated by pet lovers and Superman junkies alike. Aries was Zeus' pet who was out playing Superman one day. Being the pet of the god of the sky, Aries was special. He had golden fleece and wings so that he could fly around Mount Olympus. One day Zeus was busy eating grapes and drinking wine with one of his many love interests, when Apollo shouted for help. Apollo was looking down on the earthlings and noticed two children who had walked away from their mom when she wasn't watching. While they were sneaking around in the bushes having the time of their lives, their mom was panicking and, worse yet, a lion was stalking the kids. In a rare moment of concern for humanity, Zeus showed the scene to Aries and sent him flying down to earth to save the day. The ram zoomed down, faster than a speeding bullet, picked up the two stray children and returned them to their mother. From that day on, Aries continued to perform heroic deeds that helped the little earthlings down below. His character is quite the opposite of Zeus' other favorite pet, Aquila, who carried out the god's dirty work.

Constellation Map

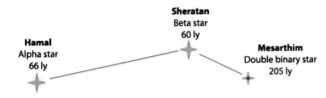

Hamal
Alpha star
66 ly

Sheratan
Beta star
60 ly

Mesarthim
Double binary star
205 ly

Smallest Constellation

Aries is such a tiny constellation that it is easy to miss. While Perseus has seventeen stars that make out an elaborate body, head and arms, and Orion has nineteen stars in his complex structure, Aries the ram is a measly three stars. They are supposed to represent a sheep's horn, but with so few stars, it is really hard to tell. Fortunately, Aries is located off by itself in a relatively dark part of the sky, so it is not confused with other constellations.

NAME
Aries is Latin for Ram.

Logan McNamee
7th grade

SPRING CONSTELLATION

The sun and moon pass through Aries from April 19-May 13. As the earth's axis changes ever so slightly, the sun's path changes, too. When the stars were mapped in 200 BC, the sun passed through Aries about one month earlier than it does today, so this constellation was assocciated with the first day of summer, the *spring equinox*.

family field guide

Auriga
The Charioteer

MONTHS IN THE SKY
November-May

OVERHEAD
February

BRIGHTEST STAR
Capella (magnitude 0.9)

FIND IT
Auriga is a giant pentagon, three fist-lengths above Orion's head. Look for the brightest star above Orion; this is Capella, the brightest star in Auriga. The pentagon is quite bright. Next, look for the three fainter stars near Capella which are the three Kids.

FUN OBSERVATIONS

ALMAAZ
This star immediately next to Capella is an ordinary looking star, but it is over 2,000 light years away! This is an example of where our depth perception fails us with stars. Capella and Almaaz appear immediately next to each other, but are separated by 1,950 light years.
Magnitude 3. 0

M36 Open cluster
These newborn stars are 30 million years old.
Magnitude 6.5

M37 Open cluster
An open cluster of several hundred newborn-stars.
Magnitude 6.0

M38 Open Cluster
These stars are estimated at 200 million years old. They are teenage stars, still moving slowly apart.
Magnitude 7.0

DECEPTION TALE   There once was a king named Oenomous and his daughter was the most beautiful girl in the kingdom. All the men wanted to marry her, so they lined up to bring her flowers, sing her songs and recite their poetry in hopes of catching her attention. The king grew tired of all this wasted time. He had the fastest horses in the kingdom, so he declared that any man who defeated him in a chariot race could marry his daughter; those who tried and failed would be killed. This didn't stop the young men from trying to win the young princess, but instead of walking away from their failed attempts, hundreds of failed chariot drivers were killed. Finally a young man named Pelops showed up. He was the son of Hermes, the messenger of the Greek gods. The gods helped him build a special chariot with wings. To ensure his victory, Pelops bribed the king's chariot driver to rig the king's chariot so that it would crash. In return, if the king was killed, Pelops would give the driver half of the kingdom. The race was on. Going around the second corner, Pelops' chariot sprouted wings and took the lead. The king's horses were fast and were slowly gaining ground when, smash, bang, boom, the wheels fell off! The driver jumped out of the chariot before it hit the wall and the king, still in the chariot, was dragged to his death. Pelops got the girl, the driver showed up to claim his half of the kingdom, and as he walked away, Pelops kicked him so hard in the back side that he flew up into the sky. While Pelops gained control of the kingdom, the chariot driver earned his place in the stars.

Constellation Map

Capella
Alpha star
42 ly

Menkalinan
Beta star
82 ly

Almaaz
2,038 ly

The Kids

M38
4,200 ly

M36, M37 and
M38 are all open
star clusters

M36
4,100 ly

M37
4,600 ly

Elnath
(part of Taurus)

THE KIDS

When I look at Auriga, I can see a house, a banged up stop sign, the Pentagon Building in Washington D.C., or even a very wide coffin, but no matter how hard I try, I cannot see a chariot driver. When they connected the same exact dots that we see today, the Greeks created a man, who happens to be a chariot driver, with a mother goat resting on his shoulder and three goat kids resting in his lap. Capella is the mother goat on the driver's shoulder and the three stars just below Capella are called "The Kids."

Valen Fey
8th grade

LATIN NAME

Auriga is the Latin word meaning "charioteer."

THE CAPELLA FOUR

The brightest star in this constellation is Capella. It is the fourth brightest star in the northern hemisphere after Sirius (part of Canis Major), Arcturus (part of Bootes) and Vega (part of Lyra and the Summer Triangle). Unlike these other bright stars, Capella is actually four stars! Two super giants, each about ten times the size of our sun, are aligned so close together that even with a moderate telescope, they appear as a single star. With a huge telescope, astronomers can see that Capella is actually four stars: the two super giants and two smaller stars.

Big Dipper

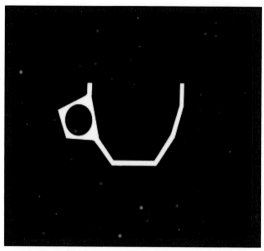

MONTHS IN THE SKY
Year-round

OVERHEAD
May

BRIGHTEST STAR
Alioth (magnitude 1.8)

FIND IT
The Big Dipper is the most commonly recognized of all the constellations. Just memorize the pattern of these bright stars and look to the northern part of the sky. This group of bright stars stands out like a sore thumb.

FUN OBSERVATIONS

POINTER STARS
An imaginary line extending from Merak through Dubhe leads to the North Star. From Dubhe, extend your arms and measure three fist-lengths to the North Star.

WHIRLPOOL GALAXY
Located just below the star Alkaid (the end of the Dipper's handle), this galaxy contains over 100 billion stars and is 50,000 light years from side to side. Because it is 37 million light years away, it appears as a speck and requires a small to medium-sized telescope. Magnitude 8.0

PINWHEEL GALAXY
Located just above Alkaid, this galaxy is twice the size of the Milky Way. Difficult to see, except in spring and summer when it is high in the sky, it still requires a telescope. Magnitude 8.2

ASTERISM A group of very smart astronomers (called the International Astronomical Union, or IAU) created a list of 88 official star constellations in 1930 and the Big Dipper is not among them. It is, however, the tail end of Ursa Major (The Great Bear), which is on the official list. The seven bright stars which make up the Big Dipper are the most easily recognizable stars in The Great Bear; the rest of the bear is difficult to find and requires a good bit of star hunting. Stars such as those in the Big Dipper, which are bright and are located close to each other, but are not an official constellation, are called an *asterism*.

THE DRINKING GOURD Slaves in the United States knew the stars well and runaways used the North Star as their guide to freedom in the northern states. The slaves commonly referred to these seven bright stars as The Drinking Gourd. Gourds are long skinny vegetables, similar to a zucchini, which were dried, hollowed out and used as ladles to "dip" for water. Their original name is likely the origin of the recent North American name, Big Dipper.

ENGLISH TRANSLATION In England this asterism is called "The Plough," which comes from their farming culture. With a bit of imagination, it is easy to see the shape of the farming tool. The two stars Alcor and Mizar (see Eye Test at right) are referred to as "the horse and rider."

family field guide

Constellation Map

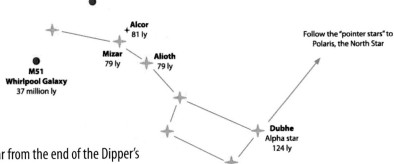

M101
Pinwheel Galaxy
27 million ly

Alcor
81 ly

Mizar
79 ly

Alioth
79 ly

M51
Whirlpool Galaxy
37 million ly

Follow the "pointer stars" to
Polaris, the North Star

Dubhe
Alpha star
124 ly

Merak
Beta star
79 ly

EYE TEST

The second star from the end of the Dipper's handle is actually a pair of stars. The brighter of these stars is called Mizar and its dim neighbor is Alcor. Look carefully to the side of Mizar and your peripheral vision should pick up the faint speck of Alcor; if not, it's time to check your prescription. These stars are not neighbors; they are several light years away from each other, and happen to line up in our siteline.

YEAR-ROUND

The Big Dipper is familiar to people living in the northern United States because it is visible every night of the year at latitudes north of 40 degrees. All stars rotate around the North Star. The Big Dipper is located very close to the North Star, so it rotates in a small circle, never dropping below the horizon.

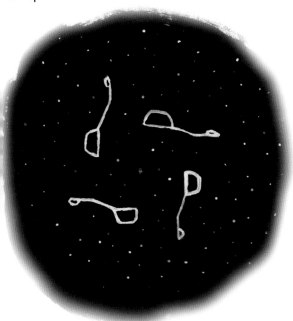

THE GREAT BEAR

The Big Dipper is a small part of Ursa Major, the Great Bear. The Dipper makes up the bear's hindquarters and tail. While most beginning stargazers have never noticed the entire constellation of Ursa Major, many civilizations have noted the Big Bear in the sky. The star Dubhe comes from an Arabic saying referring to "the back of the big bear." See the story of the Great Bear on p. 68.

Bootes
The Farmer

MONTHS IN THE SKY
March-October

OVERHEAD
June

BRIGHTEST STAR
Arcturus (magnitude -0.05)

FIND IT
Find the Big Dipper, then follow the arc of the handle three fist-lengths to the brightest star in that part of the sky, Arcturus. This is the bottom tip of the kite-shaped constellation.

FUN OBSERVATIONS
DOUBLE STARS
While there are no galaxies, nebulae or crazy star clusters in this constellation, there are quite a few interesting double stars that make for good practice with a telescope or binoculars. Scan the area of the constellation with binoculars to find at least 7 double stars in this part of the sky.

HISTORICAL NOTES
Classical Greece (500 BC-336 BC)
Many observations about the stars, planets, sun and moon had been discovered by the Egyptians and Babylonians long before the Greek civilization reached its peak. This information was shared with the Greeks so they don't get credit for "discovering" the constellations or the movements of the stars. Their great contribution to astronomy was creating mathematical calculations and detailed records that *proved* the movements of the sky objects. And, of course, they incorporated many of their stories among the stars, too.

PRONUNCIATION This constellation is not a pair of boots. It is pronounced boh-oh-tees.

THE FARMER There are several myths about Bootes, but the one I like best refers to him as a farmer and the constellation represents his plow. Bootes grew up in a nice family with a couple of good brothers, a large and successful farm and plenty of time to enjoy hunting and fishing. He did not know that he had been adopted when he was born and that his mother was the goddess of farming. In turn, he did not realize that he was a half-god living among a family of mortals. All was great until tragedy struck the farm: the parents died, the farm was given to the older brother and he stole everything, leaving Bootes broke and alone. He struggled to keep his feet under him and tried to continue farming, but it was tough work to do it all alone. He scrapped together a few sharp rocks, put together a handle to guide them and harnessed them up to his horses. *Voila*, he had designed the first plow. With this handy tool, he could turn over an entire pasture in just a couple of days. Soon, he was running one of the best farms in the village and he was running it all by himself. People began to notice his work and his crafty invention, too. Soon enough, he sold his farm and made his living building and redesigning his plow. He never once relied on the help of his goddess mother, even in tough times. In his honor, his mother placed him in the stars in the shape of the plow, the greatest early invention of farming.

Constellation Map

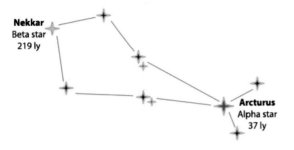

Nekkar
Beta star
219 ly

Arcturus
Alpha star
37 ly

BRIGHTEST SUMMER STAR

Arcturus is the second brightest star in the Northern Hemisphere next to Sirius, part of Canis Major. Sirius sets below the horizon in the spring, so Arcturus is the brightest star in the summer sky. To accentuate its beauty, Arcturus has a brilliant red glow. It is a red giant, over 20 times the size of our sun.

EARLY CONSTELLATION

This easy-to-find constellation was described by name in *The Odyssey*, a book written by a famous ancient Greek named Homer. The book was written over 2,000 years ago!

Jesse Ransford
7th grade

ARCTURUS' CRAZY ORBIT

Most stars in The Milky Way orbit around the galaxy's center in a similar direction, spinning along the disk of the Milky Way. Arcturus, however, is orbiting directly perpendicular to most stars. That means that it's heading our way....at a speed of about 120,000 miles per hour! Fortunately, we are not directly in its path and it will fly right past us. In a half million years it will have passed Earth and will be out of sight in the opposite direction.

Canis Major/Minor
Big Dog/Little Dog

MONTHS IN THE SKY
January-April

OVERHEAD
March

BRIGHTEST STAR
Canis Major: Sirius (magnitude -1.4)
Canis Minor: Procyon (magnitude 0.4)

FIND IT

Canis Major: Find Orion's Belt. Extend a line downward through the belt to the brightest star in the neighborhood; that is Sirius. One star to the right of Sirius is the dog's front paw. Left of Sirius is a small triangle of stars which form the tail, rear leg and back side of the big dog. It is a long constellation.

Canis Minor: Find the upper left shoulder of Orion (Betelgeuse). Next find Sirius (see above). A third bright star in the neighborhood makes the Winter Triangle. This third star, Procyon, is the heart of Canis Minor which does not look like a dog at all.

FUN OBSERVATIONS
M41
This open cluster near Canis Major has a reddish star shining in the middle. The cluster is estimated at 20 light years across. It is visible with binoculars.
Magnitude 5.0

ORION'S HUNTERS Canis Major and Canis Minor represent Orion's hunting partners. While he hated civilization and tried at all costs to avoid people, Orion never went anywhere without his loyal hunting dogs. See Orion's story on page 52. After Orion was killed by a scorpion, Artemis, goddess of the moon and of the hunt, put the loyal dogs in the sky alongside Orion.

SIRIUSLY BRIGHT Sirius is the brightest star in the entire sky, including both the Northern and Southern Hemispheres. While most visible stars have an apparent magnitude between zero and six, Sirius measures -1.4 (see p. 10 for the *apparent magnitude scale*). While it is the brightest star in the sky, it is by no means a large star. It is only twice as large as our sun, quite small compared to many stars in the sky. It appears brighter than other stars because it is "only" 8 light years away, very close compared to most stars, but still 600,000 times farther away than our sun.

GREAT DEPTH While stars appear very close together, remember that there is great depth between them. The stars in a constellation just happen to line up close together in our line of sight; they are not related in any other way. For example, Sirius, the big dog's nose, is only 8 light years away, while Aludra, the big dog's tail, is 3,200 light years away. The light we see in Sirius left the star only eight years ago, while the light from the tail star began its journey towards Earth before this dog story was even created in Ancient Greece.

Constellation Map

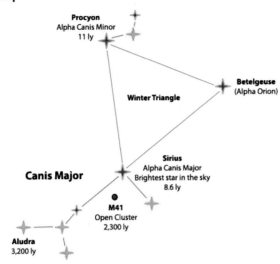

Canis Minor

Procyon
Alpha Canis Minor
11 ly

Betelgeuse
(Alpha Orion)

Winter Triangle

Canis Major

Sirius
Alpha Canis Major
Brightest star in the sky
8.6 ly

M41
Open Cluster
2,300 ly

Aludra
3,200 ly

WINTER TRIANGLE
The brightest stars in Canis Major, Canis Minor and Orion form a perfect triangle in the winter sky commonly known as the Winter Triangle.

Ruby Rappaport
8th grade

MINOR CONSTELLATION

Canis Minor, the little dog, is only one bright star and two faint stars just to the left of Orion. While it is easy to imagine Canis Major representing a dog, a good bit of imagination is needed to see this little pooch.

family field guide

Cassiopeia
The Queen

MONTHS IN THE SKY
Year-round

OVERHEAD
December

BRIGHTEST STAR
Schedar (magnitude 2.1)

FIND IT
This bright W is an outstanding constellation. Cassiopeia is located opposite the North Star from the Big Dipper. Find the Big Dipper, follow its pointer stars to the North Star (see p. 24), then continue past the North Star, and a bit to the right, to locate the W.

FUN OBSERVATIONS

M103
This open cluster was the last star feature catalogued by Charles Messier, an astronomer who identified and recorded 103 galaxies, star clusters, nebulae and other sky features. The M before the number is in reference to Messier. This cluster requires a telescope. Magnitude 7.4

M52 THE SCORPION CLUSTER
This open cluster can be seen with binoculars or a small telescope. Use the two brightest stars of Cassiopeia as pointer stars. It is half way between Cassiopeia and Cepheus. Magnitude 5.0

GREEK MYTHOLOGY Cassiopeia was the queen of Ethiopia, and was married to King Cepheus. They had a daughter named Andromeda. While Andromeda was the most beautiful woman in the kingdom, her mother, Queen Cassiopeia, was more vanity than beauty. She had the nerve to tell Poseidon that she was more beautiful than all of his wives. He didn't appreciate the lack of respect, so he snatched her daughter and had her tied to a rock beneath the sea, then hired a horrible sea monster to guard her. The Greek hero Perseus, who had recently cut the head off of the wicked Medusa, figured that if he could take on a woman whose hair was a slithering mass of snakes and whose eyes turned people to stone, he could easily take on another monster. He bargained with the king and queen that if he freed their daughter from the sea monster, he could marry Andromeda. Perseus rushed to the damsel in distress, killed the beast and saved the girl. Cepheus and Cassiopeia started planning the wedding, but just before the wedding day, another guy showed up named Phineus. He wanted to marry Andromeda too, and for some unknown reason, the king and queen decided to go back on their deal with Perseus. Perseus was mad! He returned on the wedding day with Medusa's head in his hands, held it in front of the king and queen and they were both turned to stone instantly. As a reminder of her vanity, Poseidon placed the queen in the stars, hanging upside down for half of every year as her punishment.

family field guide

Constellation Map

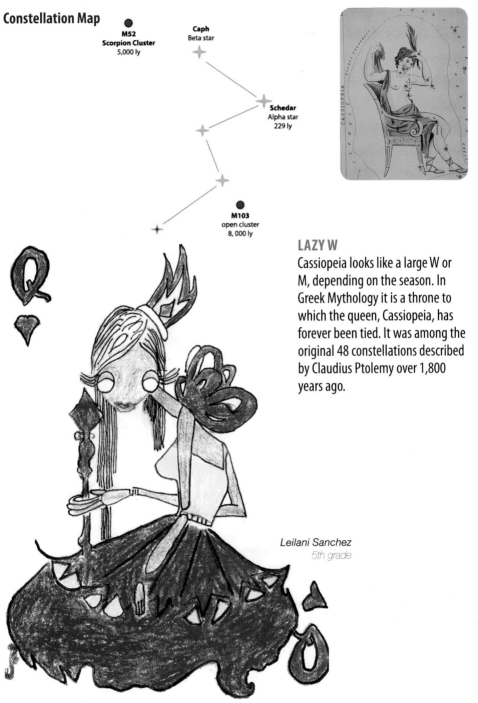

M52
Scorpion Cluster
5,000 ly

Caph
Beta star

Schedar
Alpha star
229 ly

M103
open cluster
8, 000 ly

LAZY W

Cassiopeia looks like a large W or M, depending on the season. In Greek Mythology it is a throne to which the queen, Cassiopeia, has forever been tied. It was among the original 48 constellations described by Claudius Ptolemy over 1,800 years ago.

Leilani Sanchez
5th grade

NORTHERN SKY

Because it revolves very near the North Star, Cassiopeia never goes below the horizon. It can be seen all hours of night and all seasons. Also, all seven of the stars are magnitude 2 stars, quite bright for an entire constellation. It is visible even in areas with high light pollution.

Cepheus
The King

MONTHS IN THE SKY
Year-round

OVERHEAD
October-November

BRIGHTEST STAR
Alderamin (magnitude 2.4)

FIND IT
This dim constellation requires dark skies. First, find Cassiopeia. Cepheus lies toward the open part of the W, as if the queen is embracing the king. If you still can't spot it, use the pointer stars of the Big Dipper to find the North Star. Continue past the North Star towards Cassiopeia to find the top of Cepheus' "roof."

FUN OBSERVATIONS

ERAKIS
This red giant is known as the Garnet Star and is over 5,000 light years away! It is an enormous star, but because of its great distance it is very dim. It is among the five largest stars known in the entire universe. If it were located in the sun's position, it would engulf the first five planets and nearly touch Saturn! Its brightness varies over a two year cycle ranging from magnitude 3.4, to a dimmer magnitude 4.5 (see Variable Stars at right).

DELTA CEPHEI
The star at the bottom corner of the throne, opposite Alderamin, becomes dimmer, then brighter over a 5-day cycle. It changes from a magnitude 3.6 to a dimmer 4.3. This changing brightness is called a *variable star* (see details at right).

A GENTLEMAN Cepheus was the king of Ethiopia, a great African nation. The majority of the Greek myths relating to Cepheus involve his wife Cassiopeia, whose constellation resides immediately next to him, and his daughter Andromeda. His wife loved all the attention, and she bragged constantly about her beauty (p. 30). Their daughter, Andromeda, was also the focus of much attention as Perseus fought desperately to save her from an evil sea monster (p. 56). Meanwhile, Cepheus was among them, but never did much to overshadow the two women in his life. Perhaps that is why his constellation is considerably dimmer than Cassiopeia and less magical than the galaxy that is named after his daughter. When Cassiopeia was struck down by Poseidon and cast to the stars, Cepheus remained loyal and asked Zeus to let him remain by her side. Zeus agreed and the king and queen remain together in the sky, all year long.

POLE STAR The pole star, or the North Star, is the star located directly above Earth's axis. As the earth spins, all of the stars appear to rotate around the North Star, which remains in the same place all night and all year. Over time, however, Earth's tilt shifts very slightly and the pole location changes because of this wobble. Sometimes there is no pole star at all, as in the case of the Southern Hemisphere today. Er Rai will be the pole star from the years 3000 to 5200 AD.

Constellation Map

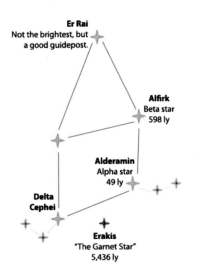

Er Rai
Not the brightest, but a good guidepost.

Alfirk
Beta star
598 ly

Alderamin
Alpha star
49 ly

Delta Cephei

Erakis
"The Garnet Star"
5,436 ly

VARIABLE STARS

The brightness of some stars changes over time. These stars are called *variable stars*. Some stars, like Erakis and Delta Cephei (see Fun Observations at left), have a pulsing behavior. Others are actually pairs of stars that orbit each other. When one star rotates in front of the other, the star appears dimmer because of an eclipse, and when they are side-by-side, they appear brighter.

Valen Fey
8th grade

RED GIANTS

One of the largest stars in the sky occurs within Cepheus, but is not one of the main seven stars of the "house." Erakis, known as the Garnet Star, is a red giant. Its old age is the cause of its massive size. Stars burn Hydrogen gas. As the Hydrogen is burned off, Helium gas builds up in the star's core. As Hydrogen supplies diminish and Helium builds up, gravity forces the Helium to contract, making the star smaller and more dense. As the pressure builds, it gets hotter and sparks up again, causing the star to get larger, and larger, and larger. These massive stars at the end of their life cycle are called *red giants*.

Coma Berenices
Berenice's Hair

MONTHS IN THE SKY
March-August

OVERHEAD
May

BRIGHTEST STAR
Al Dafirah (magnitude 4.2)

FIND IT
This constellation is dim and requires dark skies. Find the Big Dipper. Extend a line following the arc of the handle three fist-lengths to the bright red star, Arcturus. Berenice's Hair and its star cluster are half way between Arcturus and the cup of the Big Dipper.

FUN OBSERVATIONS
BERENICES CLUSTER
The most intriguing part of this constellation is the obvious star cluster which represents Queen Berenice's hair. Berenices Cluster covers a large area compared to other star clusters. An *open star cluster* is a group of stars which are all born of the same gassy material. The stars in a cluster are held together by gravitational force. Over time, the newly formed stars move slowly away from each other, and the cluster spreads outward. The stars in this cluster are quite old, born around 400 million years ago, so they have had time to move outward creating this large cluster. Magnitude 1.8

HISTORY Unlike most of the constellations in the sky, this small, dim gathering of stars is based on an actual historical event. Queen Berenice II was queen of Egypt from 246 BC-221 BC, approximately 2,250 years ago. When her husband, the king of Egypt, waged war on a group of people who had killed his sister, Queen Berenice swore to the goddess Aphrodite that she would sacrifice her long, beautiful hair if her husband returned safely. Apparently the queen was very proud of her hair and considered it among her greatest attributes. When her husband returned safely home from the battle, she cut her hair and placed it as an offering in Aphrodite's temple. The next morning, the queen's sacrifice had disappeared. The king immediately sought to find the thieves who had disrespected the offering and was ready to wage another war. The royal astronomer, whom they respected very much and sought his advice on many occasions, announced that the offering had so pleased Aphrodite, that she threw it into the stars. He pointed up to a cluster of stars and suggested that these stars were placed by Aphrodite to represent the queen's hair. They weren't officially recognized as a constellation until over 1,000 years later, but this explanation appeased the king and prevented him from waging yet another war, this one over the loss of his wife's hair.

family field guide

Constellation Map

Al Dafirah
Beta star
30 ly

Diadem
Alpha star
47 ly

Coma Berenices
Cluster

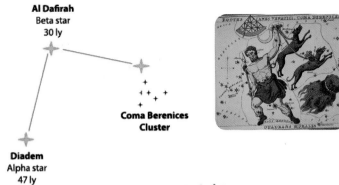

BRIGHTEST STAR

The brightest star in this constellation is similar in size and brightness to our sun. This is a good indication of just how big and bright some of the more distant stars must be. At 27 light years, a star the size of our sun is a faint star and from 50 light years away, it would not be visible to the naked eye.

Jesse Floria
7th grade

NEW CONSTELLATION

Though Berenices Cluster is quite obvious, this constellation was not recorded in early sky charts. The original constellation catalogue recorded 48 constellations, but this cluster was not included as its own constellation. Instead, it was called the Lock Of Hair, and was part of Leo's tail. Leo (p. 50) is located immediately next to Coma Berenices. Equally surprising, Charles Messier, who recorded over 100 sky objects including open star clusters, did not include Berenices Cluster in his list of interesting sky objects. Coma Berenices finally began appearing on official constellation maps in 1602, quite recently compared to most constellations which were named over 1,000 years earlier.

Corona Borealis
Northern Crown

MONTHS IN THE SKY
April-October

OVERHEAD
June

BRIGHTEST STAR
Alphecca (magnitude 2.2)

FIND IT
Find the Big Dipper. Extend a line following the arc of the handle three fist-lengths to the bright red star, Arcturus. The circle of faint stars is an obvious formation just north of Arcturus, immediately next to the big diamond of Bootes.

HISTORICAL NOTES
Mayans (2000 BC-1500 AD)
Located in Mexico and Central America, the Mayans knew the stars well and created a calendar based on their observations. Their pyramids were designed to represent this calendar with precise measurements to account for the location of the stars, sun, moon and planets. The central pyramid in Chichen Itza (in Mexico) is one example. On the first day of spring, seven triangles of sunlight shine down the north face of the staircase, like a serpent slithering down the steps.

WHOSE CROWN? An evil king named Minos ruled the island of Crete. Early in his reign, Minos' son had a successful run in the Olympic games. Shortly after, some of his close competition tricked him into fighting a bull, a contest he would most certainly lose. And he did. This made Minos furious! He was on his way to Athens to take revenge against the people of the city. Along the way, he destroyed several towns and cities. The people in Athens heard about Minos' war path and were afraid. They promised that they would do anything he asked to avoid his evil wrath.

Besides being evil, Minos had a very angry pet called the Minotaur. The Minotaur had the head of a bull and the body of a man. Minos told the people of Athens that they must send seven men and seven women every year to the Minotaur's "labyrinth," a maze with only one way in and one way out and plenty of dead ends. Each year, the people entered the maze and the Minotaur devoured them.

A great Greek hero named Theseus moved to Athens and he signed up to be sacrificed. His plan was to destroy the Minotaur and return peace to Athens. The crazy king's daughter, Ariadne, had a crush on the hero, so upon entering the Minotaur's maze, she ran down to the entrance and handed Theseus a sword and a ball of thread. He laid down the thread as he entered the maze, killed the Minotaur and followed the thread back out, like Hansel and Gretel with the bread crumbs.
(continued on next page)

Constellation Map

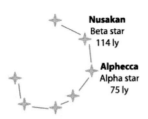

Nusakan
Beta star
114 ly

Alphecca
Alpha star
75 ly

CORONA BOREALIS GALAXY CLUSTER

A hidden cluster of galaxies resides in the southwest corner of this constellation. Don't try to find it; only professional astronomers with enormous telescopes can detect it. It is estimated at over 1 billion light years away and some guess that it contains over 400 different galaxies, all within the width of your pinky finger held straight out toward the sky. Even though most of us will never see it, just knowing that such vast space exists is an incredible statement on the size of creation.

WHOSE CROWN? (CONTINUED)

Outside the arena, Theseus met up with Ariadne, ran to the sea, hopped on a sailboat and sailed off to a remote Greek island together. You'd think they would live happily ever after, right? Wrong. Ariadne must have been a really bad traveling partner; while she slept on the beach, Theseus took off, leaving her alone on the island. Lucky for her, the Greek god of wine, Dionysus, happened to be vacationing there and they enjoyed a few bottles of the finest wines together. After hearing her story, the god felt sorry for her and threw a princess' crown into the sky for all to remember.

Corvus
The Crow

MONTHS IN THE SKY
April-July

OVERHEAD
Remains low in the southern sky

BRIGHTEST STAR
Gienah (magnitude 2.6)

FIND IT
Corvus is immediately next to Virgo. Extend a line from the handle of the Big Dipper three fist-lengths to the bright twinkling star, Arcturus. Continue that line to the next brightest star, Spica, the brightest star in Virgo. Corvus is a dim trapezoid just to the right of Spica.

HISTORICAL NOTES

Australian Aborigines (48,000 BC-- present) The native tribes of Australia have a tremendous history dating back as far as 50,000 years, longer than any other single group of people. Some estimate that they are the earliest astronomers. They were nomadic people who did not build permanent structures like the Egyptians or the Mayans, but their rock art shows an understanding of the stars as a primary tool in guiding their migration patterns and their relationships with seasonal animal behaviors. The earliest known rock engravings date back 45,000 years.

OLD CROW According to this Greek myth, crows have not always been the black birds with the raspy *caw* which we know today. Instead, they had brilliant white feathers and golden wings and their song was the most brilliant of all the birds. All that changed with Corvus, who served the Greek god Apollo. Apollo sent his trusted crow out with an empty cup to collect water from a secret fountain that poured the tastiest of water. Along the way Corvus met some friends. He stopped for a short visit with his buddies, then, being the most sociable of animals, he forgot all about his mission and stayed out all night. He woke up lost and confused and could not remember the location of the fountain. He finally gave up his mission and started back to Olympus. Along the way he thought up all kinds of excuses to explain why he was returning with an empty cup. He told Apollo that he was attacked by a snake and the venomous bite left him confused and bewildered. Apollo didn't fall for the sneaky little lie and cursed all crows by taking away their brilliant colors and their beautiful song. He turned them pure black and placed in their throats the raspy call that we know today. In his anger, Apollo threw Corvus up into the stars and he placed two other constellations nearby, Hydra the snake, and Crater, the empty cup. Corvus can forever see the serpent that struck him and the empty water cup which leaves him thirsty with that raspy old voice (these constellations are not included in this guide).

family field guide

Constellation Map

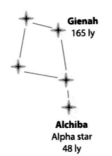

Gienah
165 ly

Alchiba
Alpha star
48 ly

OLD CONSTELLATION

While Corvus is a small constellation, it was one of the original 48 star pictures recorded by Claudius Ptolemy.

ALTERNATE STORY

Another of the Crow's stories in Greek mythology shares similar bad luck for the poor bird. Apollo trusted his faithful crow to watch over his pregnant wife, to ensure her safety, and that of their coming son. She slowly lost interest in Apollo and became attracted to a mortal man. Instead of punishing his wife or the man who stole her, Apollo turned the bird black and took away its voice, making all crows forever dark and raspy.

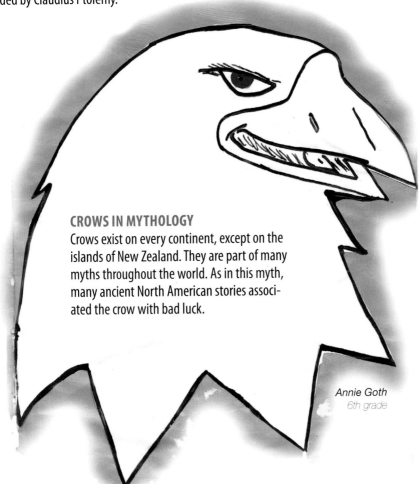

CROWS IN MYTHOLOGY

Crows exist on every continent, except on the islands of New Zealand. They are part of many myths throughout the world. As in this myth, many ancient North American stories associated the crow with bad luck.

Annie Goth
6th grade

Cygnus
The Swan

MONTHS IN THE SKY
June-December

OVERHEAD
September

BRIGHTEST STAR
Deneb (magnitude 1.25)

FIND IT
Find the three bright stars in the summer and fall sky that make up the Summer Triangle. Of these three stars, Deneb, the swan's tail star, is the northern-most and is among the haze of the Milky Way. Look for the cross which forms the wings, then the dimmer star Albireo which completes the swan's long neck.

FUN OBSERVATIONS

DENEB
The tail star, over 1,500 light years away, is an enormous star, over 200 times the size of the sun and 60,000 times brighter. It is the farthest magnitude 1 star from Earth. Magnitude 1.2

COATHANGER CLUSTER
Officially, this cluster is called Brocchi's Cluster. Its brightest stars take the shape of a coathanger. Though these stars appear like an open cluster, they are great distances apart and happen to line up in our sightline. Magnitude 5.1

NORTH AMERICA NEBULA
Stars behind this gassy mass create a cloud-like appearance. In telescopes you can see the shape of the North American continent. Very dark skies are needed for good viewing. Magnitude 4.0

CRAZY CHARIOT DRIVER The original story of Cygnus is unknown for certain and there are great differences even among the most popular versions of this story. My favorite of the Cygnus stories involves Apollo, the god of the sun. His job was to drive his sun chariot across the sky each day. His son, Phaethon, really admired his dad and was always eyeing his sweet ride. He frequently asked if he could take the chariot out for a drive across the sky some day, but was constantly denied. As happens to the best of us, Apollo slept a bit late one morning and Phaethon stepped in to save the day. He hopped in the chariot, and started across the sky. Unfortunately, he didn't have the proper training and he quickly lost control. Zeus noticed the crazy, haphazard path of the sun chariot, then realized that Apollo was still sleeping. He quickly woke the sun god, and Apollo shot out of bed to grab the moon chariot from his sister's garage. He began chasing his hijacked chariot across the sky, not knowing who was at the wheel up ahead of him. Meanwhile, Zeus shot a lightning bolt at the hijacked ride and hit Phaethon, knocking him out of the chariot sending him earthward where he landed in a river down below. Apollo managed to get the sun chariot back under control and didn't realize until later that his son was the driver and victim of this tragic misunderstanding. In memory of Phaethon's dive into the river, his body was placed in the sky as a swan. Cygnus is the Latin word for swan.

Constellation Map

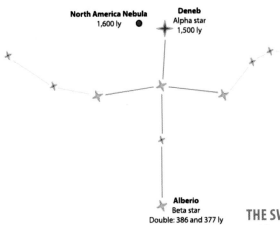

North America Nebula
1,600 ly ●

Deneb
Alpha star
1,500 ly

Alberio
Beta star
Double: 386 and 377 ly

THE SWAN
Unlike many constellations, Cygnus actually looks like the animal that it represents. Deneb, the brightest star in the constellation is Arabic for "tail." A straight line from Deneb following the Milky Way leads to the beak, a relatively bright double star called Albireo. The wings span a perpendicular line across the body, each of which extends back towards the tail.

FLYING THE MILKY WAY
Cygnus flies among the cloudy mass of the Milky Way throughout summer, fall and into early winter.

Aeelyn Villacarra
7th grade

THE NORTHERN CROSS
One of the brightest and most famous constellations in the Southern Hemisphere is the Southern Cross. Within Cygnus is a similar, though much larger cross, called the Northern Cross. The five brightest stars of Cygnus make up the *asterism*, a small part of the larger constellation.

Delphinus
The Dolphin

MONTHS IN THE SKY
July-December

OVERHEAD
October

BRIGHTEST STAR
Rotanev (magnitude 3.6)

FIND IT
This small, faint constellation requires a dark sky. Find the three bright stars in the summer and fall sky that make up the Summer Triangle. The southern-most of these stars is Altair, part of Aquila. Delphinus is one fist-length east of Altair.

FUN OBSERVATIONS

ROTANEV
The brightest star in the constellation is a visual double star. While the two stars appear very close together, they are actually many light years apart; they happen to line up close together in a our sightline.
Magnitude 4.0 and 4.9

GAMMA DELPHI
The tip of the dolphin's nose is another double star. The brighter of the two stars has a gold color, while its partner appears bluish-green.
Magnitude 4.5 and 5.5

THE MYTH As with most myths, there are many disputed versions of which is the real story of Delphinus. My favorite involves an ancient rock star named Arion. Arion the rock star was the most popular guy of his time. He was the Bono of the Greek generation. Unfortunately for him, he was a tight wad. While he was making big money and living the good life, he didn't share his wealth with his support team. The roadies and tour crew lived in poverty, while he was indulging in the finer things of life. After a while, his support team had enough of his stinginess. While sailing to a concert, the ship's crew organized a revolt and they forced him to walk the plank into the shark-filled ocean. His last request was to play one final song to the world. They threw him his harp (the Greek version of a Gibson electric guitar) and allowed him to play one last song. As he played, the dolphins of the ocean approached the ship to hear his song. Finally, as the song came to a close, he leaped into the depths. The largest of the dolphins rescued the poet, swam him back to the mainland and the gods were so pleased to have preserved the musical genius that they honored the dolphin in the stars.

DELPHINUS Delphinus is the Latin word meaning Dolphin. This is one constellation in which you can actually imagine the shape of a dolphin with its curling tail swimming in the sky.

family field guide

Constellation Map

Sualocin
Alpha star
241 ly

Rotanev
Beta star
97 ly

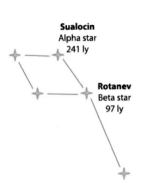

THE NAMING OF STARS

The brightest stars of Delphinus are named after Nicolaus Venator, an assistant to the head astronomer in an Italian observatory when the names of these stars were published in 1814. He didn't make any significant discoveries, he just happened to hold a good job when the star names were published, and his name is spelled out backwards in these two stars.

Tristan Lane
8th grade

SEEING DIM STARS

Delphinus is not a bright constellation. Surprisingly, it appears brighter when looking just to the side of the shimmering stars than when looking directly at them. Within our eyes are two different kinds of cells, called *rods* and *cones*. Cones are built to see bright colors and they are packed tightly in the center of each eye. Rods detect very dim light. They don't do much work during the bright daytime hours, but they kick in at night and are located mostly on the edges of the eye. Because of the location of the rods, dim stars appear brighter through our peripheral vision.

Draco
The Dragon

MONTHS IN THE SKY
Year-round

OVERHEAD
August

BRIGHTEST STAR
Eltanin (magnitude 2.2)

FIND IT
First, find Vega, the brightest star in the Summer Triangle and part of Lyra. Look two fist-lengths north to a trapezoid of stars which form Draco's head. From there, find the two brightest stars pointing directly towards the tip of Cepheus. The next star is directly west, then the next two stars curve directly towards Arcturus, the brightest star in Bootes. Finally, curve back towards the handle of the Big Dipper. The body slithers between the Big Dipper's handle and the cup of the Little Dipper. Two more stars extend between the two bears to complete the tail.

HISTORICAL NOTES
Ancient Egypt (3000 BC-2000 BC)
Located in northern Africa, the Egyptians used the stars in both their calendar and in building their pyramids. The pyramids are aligned almost perfectly, facing the cardinal directions; directly north, south, east and west. Star charts which relate to their calendar have been identified within the coffin lids of several pharaohs. They also knew that when Sirius, the brightest star in the sky, began to rise on the horizon, the Nile River would begin to flood, marking the beginning of a new planting cycle that sustained their entire civilization.

THE LEGEND Hera was Zeus' wife. As the queen of the gods, she was an important woman in Greek mythology and she needed good protection. Her bodyguard was a dragon named Draco. On their wedding day, Zeus gave Hera a basket of golden apples. Hera loved her apples very much and assigned Draco to guard them, her most precious possession. While Draco was busy guarding the golden apples, the Greek hero Hercules was being punished for killing his wife. He was assigned to complete twelve tasks in order to be forgiven for his crime. One of his tasks was to steal the golden apples. It took quite a bit of daring for Hercules to sneak into Hera's garden, but he did it and almost got away easily. Unfortunately for our hero, Draco realized the intruder's presence and whacked him in the face with that extremely long tail. They continued to battle for hours before Hercules finally killed the faithful dragon. Hercules got away with the apples and moved onto his twelfth and final task, while Hera, in her sadness, threw Draco up into the heavens, sprawling him out among the northern constellations.

YEAR ROUND Because it is located so near to the North Star, Draco is visible throughout the entire year, though it dips very low to the horizon in winter. Summer is the best time to see this hard-to-find constellation.

family field guide

Constellation Map

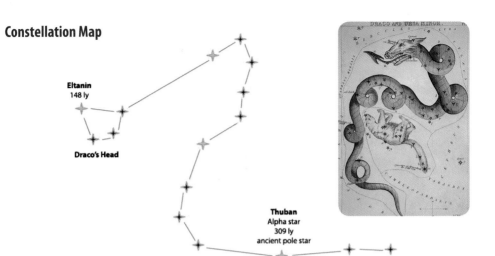

Eltanin
148 ly

Draco's Head

Thuban
Alpha star
309 ly
ancient pole star

ANCIENT NORTH STAR

The pole star, or North Star, is located directly above Earth's axis point. As the earth spins, all of the stars appear to move, except for the pole star which stays in one spot. Today, the pole star is located in the handle of the Little Dipper. But, over time, the earth wobbles just a little and its axis point changes ever so slightly. This change in the axis means that the pole star changes, too. Thousands of years ago, civilizations noted Thuban as the pole star.

Courtnay Edwards
7th grade

EGYPTIANS

The Egyptians understood a lot about astronomy and had elaborate records of the stars, the sun and the moon. They used this information in many ways, one of which was to guide their rituals. An essential part of their rituals was to ensure that the pharaohs traveled safely in the afterlife. Archaeologists discovered two holes piercing directly through the burial chamber in one of the Great Pyramids in Giza. For years, they assumed that these were air shafts, but later realized that one of the holes looked directly at the ancient pole star. As the pole star of its time, Thuban stayed in one spot in the sky. Thuban was the timeless, unchanging guide for the burial ceremony and served as the caretaker of the pharaoh's journey into eternity.

Gemini
The Twins

MONTHS IN THE SKY
December-May

OVERHEAD
March

BRIGHTEST STAR
Pollox (magnitude 1.1)

FIND IT
Look for the two equally bright stars to the upper left of Orion; these are Castor and Pollux, the brightest stars in Gemini. Next, look for the two nearly-parallel lines of stars dropping from each of these bright stars; these are the twins.

FUN OBSERVATIONS
M35
This open cluster is large and bright and is easily visible with binoculars.
Magnitude 5.5

HISTORICAL NOTES
Anasazi (50-1450 AD)
Located in the Southwestern region of North America (Colorado, Utah, Arizona and New Mexico), the Anasazi people were a group of cave dwelling tribes whose lasting records remain as rock carvings and paintings. One site shows what is thought to record a supernova explosion which created the Crab Nebula in 1054 AD (see p. 67). This same event was recorded by Chinese astronomers and others throughout the world. Besides their rock art records, they built an observatory on top of a mesa called Hovenweep Castle in the Four Corners area.

BROTHERS AND FRIENDS Castor and Pollux were twin brothers. Their mother was the Queen of Sparta, a mortal woman. Strange as it may seem, and impossible as we know it, they had different fathers. We'll just say that nine months before they were born, their mother was with two different guys, one of which was very likely Zeus, the leader of the gods...such is the nature of Greek mythology. Anyway, Castor's father was a mortal man and Pollux's father was Zeus. They did not know that they had different fathers and that one of them was mortal while the other was immortal. Like many siblings, believe it or not, Castor and Pollux were best friends. They did everything together and were both very talented fellas. One was a great horseman, the other a great boxer. One night, they got entangled in a fight with two other guys and the brothers won the scuffle. Unfortunately, Castor, the mortal, took a sword blade to the side and got a nasty infection, resulting in his death. Pollux, Zeus' son, missed him so much that he wanted to die so that he could join his brother in the underworld. Being half god, he was immortal and could not die. After much begging and pleading, Zeus made the arrangement that Pollux could spend half of each day in the underworld with his brother and half the day walking among the living. Zeus was so impressed by the loyalty of the twins that he placed them in the sky together, two of the brightest stars in the region of Orion throughout the winter months.

Constellation Map

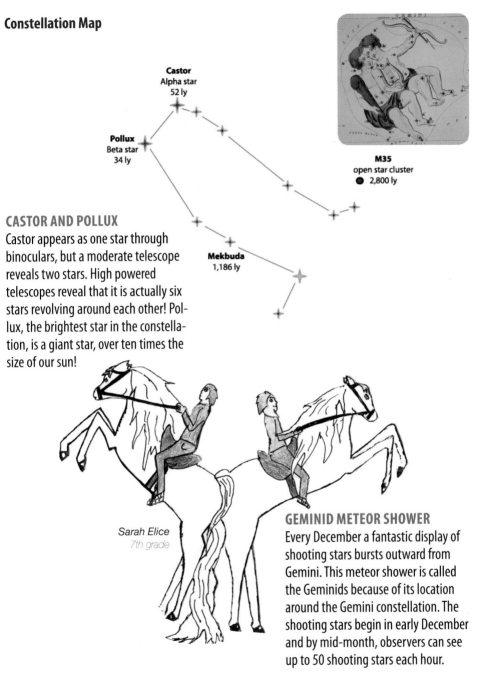

Castor
Alpha star
52 ly

Pollux
Beta star
34 ly

M35
open star cluster
● 2,800 ly

Mekbuda
1,186 ly

CASTOR AND POLLUX

Castor appears as one star through binoculars, but a moderate telescope reveals two stars. High powered telescopes reveal that it is actually six stars revolving around each other! Pollux, the brightest star in the constellation, is a giant star, over ten times the size of our sun!

Sarah Elice
7th grade

GEMINID METEOR SHOWER

Every December a fantastic display of shooting stars bursts outward from Gemini. This meteor shower is called the Geminids because of its location around the Gemini constellation. The shooting stars begin in early December and by mid-month, observers can see up to 50 shooting stars each hour.

SAILOR'S OMEN

Ancient European sailors used the stars as their guide, not only for navigation, but also for predicting seasonal patterns. When these ancient sea-goers began to see Gemini rising in the sky just before dawn, they knew that the awful storms of winter had passed, and they could count on calmer seas as summer approached.

Hercules
The Hero

MONTHS IN THE SKY
May-November

OVERHEAD
July

BRIGHTEST STAR
Kornephoros (magnitude 2.7)

FIND IT
Hercules can be difficult to find as the stars in the core are quite dim. Use the stars of the Summer Triangle as a guide. A cock-eyed square, the hero's body, is located between Vega, the brightest star in the Summer Triangle, and Arcturus, the brightest star in the summer sky.

FUN OBSERVATIONS
M13 GLUBULAR CLUSTER
Through binoculars, this appears as a small whisp of smoke against a black sky. In fact, it is hundreds of thousands of stars packed tightly together, held there by strong gravitational forces, over 25,000 light years away. These are some of the oldest stars in the sky (see Star Clusters at right). Some astronomers estimate the age of this cluster at 13 billion years old, meaning that they have existed since the beginning of our universe!
Magnitude 7.0

RASALGETHI
With a small telescope, you can see a double star; one star is orange, the other is bluish. Binoculars are not strong enough to separate the two stars.
Magnitude 2.8

HERCULES THE HERO? Hercules could be called a dishonorable hero. He was a hero because he worked his entire life to be forgiven for a horrific crime and he is dishonorable for his original crime. He was married to a nice young gal and they got along for a number of years. After a while it seemed that Hercules couldn't do anything to please his girl and no matter how hard he tried, she found problems with him. One night she must have scolded him for leaving his dishes out on the counter after dinner. This was the last straw for Hercules. In a fit of rage, he killed her. He immediately felt awful for his crime. He asked forgiveness of his wife's father who was also the king. Rather than sending him to his death, the king set 12 virtually impossible tasks for Hercules to fulfill. He was asked to kill a dreadful lion (Leo), a 9-headed serpent, a sacred deer, a powerful bull, a watchful dragon (Draco), a tempermental wild pig, a monster's herd of cattle, a band of man-eating horses, a flock of man-eating birds and more. Hercules spent his entire life fulfilling his promise and earning the king's forgiveness, and was ultimately recognized by the gods as they placed him in the sky. His original crime was forgiven, but not forgotten and so they hung him upside down among the heavens. Because of the nearly impossible tasks which he fulfilled, people today refer to incredible feats of strength and courage as "herculean tasks."

Constellation Map

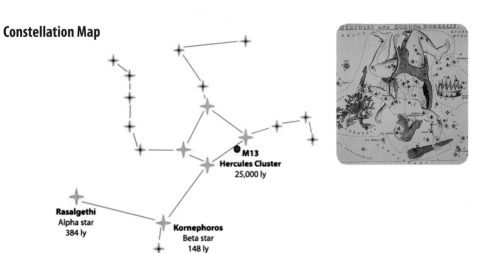

M13
Hercules Cluster
25,000 ly

Rasalgethi
Alpha star
384 ly

Kornephoros
Beta star
148 ly

HERO OR PINWHEEL

Upon finding the trapezoid that is the body of Hercules, I first see a guy dancing with his arms swinging up in the air and his legs kicked up in a little jig. At second glance, I see a pinwheel of arms spinning around the body. The original pictures of the hero, though, depict him kneeling upside down with a club over his head, thrusting forth a bouquet of serpents.

Chapin Newhard
8th grade

STAR CLUSTERS

Within the night sky there are small pockets of star clusters. There are two different types of star clusters. *Open clusters* are places where new stars have just been born. They are born of a collection of hydrogen gases that are held together by gravity and have caught fire. Though the gravity is still holding these new stars together, they are slowly pulling apart and moving outward. *Globular clusters* are the exact opposite of open clusters; they are a gathering place of very, very old stars that are held so tightly by gravitational force that they never dispersed. The cluster is very dense and the stars can be billions of years old, without ever having left their sibling stars.

Leo
The Lion

MONTHS IN THE SKY
February-July

OVERHEAD
April-May

BRIGHTEST STAR
Regulus (magnitude 1.3)

FIND IT
Leo's head, shaped like a backwards question mark, is the key to finding this bright constellation. Find the Big Dipper. A line drawn between the two stars at the end of the Dipper, through the bottom of the cup (opposite of the North Star), leads to Leo's head, formerly known as The Sickle.

FUN OBSERVATIONS
BEEHIVE CLUSTER
This large open cluster is barely visible with the naked eye on dark nights. Located just to the right of Leo's head, this large cluster contains about fifty stars over an area twice the size of the moon.
Magnitude 4.0

HISTORICAL NOTES
Pawnee Tribe (North America)
Traditionally located in the grasslands of Nebraska, the Pawnee tribe were not a nomadic tribe. They built permanent houses and their design was based on astronomical observation. The villages were laid out in the position of the most important stars in the sky. The doors of the lodges always faced east to the rising sun. The four posts represented the four directions (exactly northwest, northeast, southwest and southeast). The domed roof represented the dome of the evening sky.

HERCULEAN MYTH Leo was an enormous lion who terrorized the people in the countryside villages. His hide was so thick that no spear or arrow could pierce it. He was enormous and mean and he ate innocent people for lunch. The king wanted to protect his people from that darned pest, but could never figure out how to get the job done. It just happened that his daughter was married to a man named Hercules. Their marriage started out well enough, but after some time he could never do anything right. She complained to him when he took the garbage out when the can was only half-full, and she complained when he didn't take it out because it stunk up the house. One day, he had enough of her complaints. As was the way of things back then....he killed her. Hercules realized that he'd done wrong and asked the king, his wife's father, for forgiveness. The king gave Hercules 12 seemingly impossible tasks to complete in order to be forgiven. The first task on the list was to kill Leo and forever bring peace to the countryside. Hercules went out into hills, without any weapons at all, and stalked the great lion. He climbed up a tree and waited for the lion to lie down to rest. When all was quiet, Hercules leaped out of the tree, onto Leo's back and strangled the beast with his bare hands. He skinned the animal with its own claws and wore its head as a helmet and returned victorious. Once all twelve of Hercules' tasks had been accomplished, the gods placed him and his first victim in the sky.

family field guide

Constellation Map

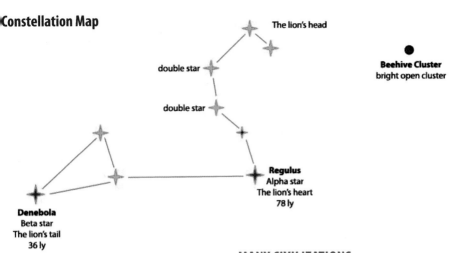

The lion's head

Beehive Cluster
bright open cluster

double star

double star

Regulus
Alpha star
The lion's heart
78 ly

Denebola
Beta star
The lion's tail
36 ly

LOST TAIL

An Egyptian astronomer in 240 BC chopped off Leo's tail! The constellation now known as Coma Berenices was once part of Leo's tail. See the story of Coma Berenices (p. 34) to discover how Leo lost his tail.

MANY CIVILIZATIONS

Leo is one of the original 48 constellations recorded by Claudius Ptolemy over 1,800 years ago. Even before this official record, many civilizations related these stars to the lion. The Persians (modern-day Iran), the Turks, the Syrians, the Jews and the Indians of India all had names for this constellation which referred to the lion. Even the brightest star's name, Regulus, means *little king*, in referene to the king of the beasts.

Aeelyn Villacarra
7th grade

NEAR STAR

The star called Wolf 359 is located just below and to the right of Regulus. It is the closest Northern Hemisphere star to our solar system, and the third closest star in the entire sky. It is only 7.7 light years away, but is one of the smallest and dimmest of all stars and is only visible with a professional telescope. See its size comparison on page 15.

Lyra
The Lyre

MONTHS IN THE SKY
May-December

OVERHEAD
September

BRIGHTEST STAR
Vega (magnitude 0.0)

FIND IT
First find Vega, the brightest star of the Summer Triangle (p. 64). This brightest star is the end of a tail, which connects to four dim stars in the form of a small diamond or a kite. The diamond is the harp.

FUN OBSERVATIONS
EPSILON LYRA
Immediately above Vega, you can see a double star through binoculars. With a small telescope you can see that there are actually four stars. A pair of stars which orbit each other is called a *binary pair*; a pair of doubles is called a double-double. Here we have two sets of stars orbiting each other and the pairs orbit each other as well. Though they are all held together by gravity, there is a distance of some 1 trillion miles between the most distant stars in this group. Magnitude 4.0 and 5.0

M57 THE RING NEBULA
Through a small telescope, this feature appears as a whisp of smoke (it cannot be seen through binoculars). In fact, it is a star that is coming to the end of its life and is blowing off a shell of gas that encompasses several light years of space (see Planetary Nebula at right). Magnitude 8.0

LOVE'S TRAGEDY Orpheus was a famous musician. He was also the son of Apollo, the god of the sun and of the arts. In the same way that women were driven to tears and shrieks of joy when watching the Beatles in the 1960s, Orpheus' music was so inspirational that he, too, charmed all who heard his work, even the rocks, trees and rivers. One lucky audience member, the Yoko Ono of the age, charmed Orpheus in return. Her name was Eurydice. One day, another man began flirting with Eurydice, but the faithful woman ran from him. As she ran, a snake reared its ugly head and bit her with venomous fangs. She died instantly and was taken to the underworld. Orpheus was so desperate to have her back that he went down into the underworld and convinced the rulers there to give Eurydice another chance to live. They accepted his plea and told him that she could follow him up to the land of the living, and as long as he did not look back, she could rejoin him there. As they were making the long journey out, their pace became slow and they both grew hungry. Just as they were about to emerge among the living, Orpheus looked back to see that his love was alright and she immediately disappeared. She made no complaint of her husband as it was an instinct of love that made him look back to see that she was alright. Orpheus' life was never the same; he never recovered from losing his love twice and Zeus placed his harp in the stars in memory of Orpheus' musical genius and his lost love.

Constellation Map

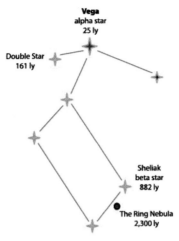

Vega
alpha star
25 ly

Double Star
161 ly

Sheliak
beta star
882 ly

The Ring Nebula
2,300 ly

PLANETARY NEBULAE

Stars look like they are just sitting there, burning away in the sky, but they are constantly changing in ways that scientists can observe and study. The Ring Nebula is a star which is getting to the end of its life and is "burping" out heaps of gas. As the light shines through the gas, it appears as a halo of light surrounding the dying star. This backlit gassy burp is called a *planetary nebula*.

ANCIENT HARP

Lyra is Latin for lyre, an ancient stringed instrument similar to a harp.

Annie Goth
6th grade

VEGA

Vega is the second brightest star in the summer sky, next to Arcturus (constellation Bootes). Besides our own sun, Vega is perhaps the most studied star in the solar system. It was the first star photographed by astronomers at the Harvard Observatory in 1850 and to this day it gets a lot of attention. One current investigation is the study of a disc of dust surrounding Vega. Astronomers wonder if there is a planetary system, much like our own, evolving around the star.

Orion
The Hunter

MONTHS IN THE SKY
December-April

OVERHEAD
February

BRIGHTEST STAR
Rigel (magnitude 0.1)

FIND IT
As the largest and brightest constellation in the winter sky, Orion is the easiest winter constellation to find. Look for the three obvious stars lined up diagonally; this is Orion's Belt. Four stars create a large, box-like perimeter around the Belt; these are Orion's shoulders and feet.

FUN OBSERVATIONS
M42 THE GREAT ORION NEBULA
This *emission nebula* is a huge cloud of hydrogen gas where new stars are in the process of being born. With binoculars or a small telescope, you can actually see four stars already burning bright. They are in a trapezoid shape, called the Trapezium.
Magnitude 5.0

HISTORICAL NOTES
Incas (1000-1575 AD)
The city of Cuzco, in modern day Peru, South America, was the center of the Incan empire and was laid out according to astronomical events. Tall pillars were built around the city and when the sun rose or set between these pillars, the leaders knew that it was time to plant or harvest at specific altitudes within the Andes mountains.

MORTAL HUNTER Orion was a hunter who wanted a solitary life in the woods. To avoid other humans, he hunted at night, and to further ensure his privacy, he lived on a deserted island. Artemis, the goddess of the moon and of the hunt, drove her moon chariot across the sky each night, and she began to take notice of Orion, hunting alone on his island. She watched him each night and became increasingly curious. Though she knew it was not alright, she decided to drop down to the island for a quick visit. Of course, it was love at first sight for both of them. She still had to drag the moon across the sky, but each night she stopped by to join him in his hunt. As luck would have it, Zeus, her uncle and the king of the gods, found out about these nightly visits and he was less than pleased. He planned to drop an enormous scorpion down onto the island to kill the hunter and improve Artemis' sense of duty. On the night of the assassination, his dogs woke Orion from his midday snooze just as the scorpion was about to strike. A long battle ensued and just as Orion was about to make the final blow against the scorpion, Artemis began to rise in the sky. Orion lost his focus, looked up to see Artemis and the scorpion made its death strike. Artemis arrived on the scene too late. In her sorrow, she threw both Orion and the scorpion into opposite parts of the sky. As Orion rises in the sky in early winter, Scorpius descends the other side of the horizon, so they will never encounter each other again.

Constellation Map

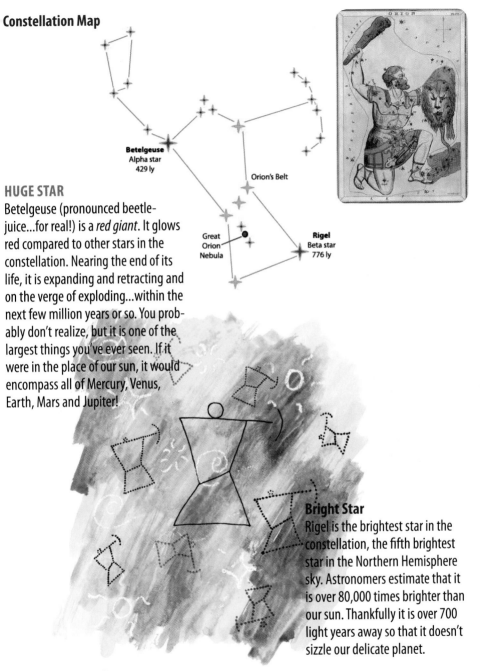

Betelgeuse
Alpha star
429 ly

Orion's Belt

Great
Orion
Nebula

Rigel
Beta star
776 ly

HUGE STAR

Betelgeuse (pronounced beetle-juice...for real!) is a *red giant*. It glows red compared to other stars in the constellation. Nearing the end of its life, it is expanding and retracting and on the verge of exploding...within the next few million years or so. You probably don't realize, but it is one of the largest things you've ever seen. If it were in the place of our sun, it would encompass all of Mercury, Venus, Earth, Mars and Jupiter!

Bright Star

Rigel is the brightest star in the constellation, the fifth brightest star in the Northern Hemisphere sky. Astronomers estimate that it is over 80,000 times brighter than our sun. Thankfully it is over 700 light years away so that it doesn't sizzle our delicate planet.

EMISSION NEBULA

Just below Orion's Belt is the Great Orion Nebula. It is a huge cloud of Hydrogen gas where new stars are being born. An *emission nebula* is a cloud of gas in which new stars light up the cloud causing the gases to glow. Through binoculars or a small telescope, infant stars are visible within the gassy cloud; these baby stars are only 10-20 million years old.

Pegasus
The Flying Horse

MONTHS IN THE SKY
August-February

OVERHEAD
November

BRIGHTEST STAR
Markab (magnitude 2.4)

FIND IT
First, locate Cassiopeia (p. 28). The corners of the W point toward Pegasus, about two fist-lengths away. Look for the huge open square which is Pegasus' body. The top right corner of the Great Square makes up the head. Stars extending from Markab make the front legs. The parallel lines extending from Alpheratz make the wings and Andromeda, the rider.

FUN OBSERVATIONS

M31 ANDROMEDA GALAXY
Only visible in very dark skies, this is the most distant light visible with the naked eye. At 2.5 million light years away, binoculars make it appear as a cloud of dust. In fact, it is an entire galaxy of over a trillion stars that extend over 150,000 light years from edge to edge! Magnitude 4.3

M15
At 33,000 ly away, this globular cluster contains several million stars! Through binoculars it is barely visible as a tiny whispy cloud. Magnitude 6.2

GREEK MYTH Instead of watching movies or television, the Greeks relied on storytellers to share the legends of their heroes, their villains, their gods and their culture, using the stars as their tool. The story of Pegasus and Andromeda is a continuation of the soap opera involving the constellations of Cassiopeia, Cepheus and Perseus. While Cassiopeia is the mischievous woman that is so easy to hate, Cepheus is the father who watches all the action from the sidelines, Andromeda is the poor heroine and Pegasus is her rescuer. This story picks up in the middle of the Cassiopeia story (p. 30) in which Andromeda is chained to a rock and is being guarded by the horrible sea monster, Cetus. She is trying to escape as the chains clang, clang against the boulder, when suddenly Perseus, the hero, flies into the scene wearing Mercury's winged shoes. Having just cut the head off of Medusa, whose icy stare turns everything into stone, Perseus holds the head up in front of Cetus and turns the monster into stone. As he turns away, a drop of blood from Medusa's shredded neck drips into the ocean, and, as if by a magic that only the Greeks could produce, a winged horse was created that answered to all of Perseus' commands. Pegasus, the winged horse, flew to the beach and chewed through the chains, freed Andromeda from her doom and carried her back to her hero, to whom she was later married. The gods so loved this story, they place Andromeda riding upon Pegasus in the night sky.

family field guide

Constellation Map

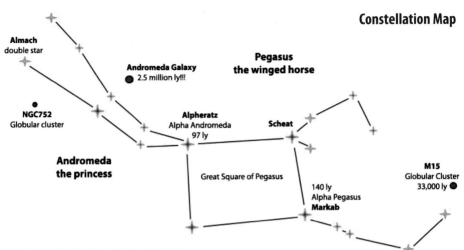

Almach
double star

Andromeda Galaxy
● 2.5 million ly!!!

Pegasus
the winged horse

NGC752
Globular cluster

Alpheratz
Alpha Andromeda
97 ly

Scheat

Andromeda
the princess

Great Square of Pegasus

140 ly
Alpha Pegasus
Markab

M15
Globular Cluster
33,000 ly ●

FINDING THE ANDROMEDA GALAXY

To find the Andromeda Galaxy, the most distant point of light visible with the naked eye, first find Cassiopeia, the W. Next find the parallel lines of Pegasus' wings. The tiny whisp of light is half-way between Cassiopeia and Pegasus' wings. The points of the W point toward the distant galaxy.

SHARING A STAR

Alpheratz is a shared star in two constellations. It is the second brightest star in the Great Square of Pegasus, and is recognized as the brightest star in Andromeda. It is the pointer star to the string of equally bright stars which make up Andromeda.

Erin Spence
8th grade

AUTUMN'S SQUARE

Pegasus dominates the night sky in fall as The Great Square of Pegasus covers quite a large space. With a little imagination, you can actually see the flying horse. The Great Square is its body, its head and neck form a little triangle off the corner of Scheat. Its front leg extends forward as if he is pumping the double-jointed limb just below his head. The wings extend opposite its head off of Alpheratz, in two nearly parallel lines. Officially, the lower parallel line is Pegasus' wing, while the uppermost parallel is Andromeda, the rider.

family field guide

Perseus
The Hero

MONTHS IN THE SKY
October-April

OVERHEAD
December

BRIGHTEST STAR
Mirfak (magnitude 1.8)

FIND IT
First, locate Cassiopeia (p. 30). Just below the W, about one fist-length away following the path of the Milky Way, look for the dim triangle of stars which is Persues' head. Trail downward, away from Cassiopeia, to a series of brighter stars which is Perseus' body, then off to the right for Algol, Medusa's head.

FUN OBSERVATIONS

ALGOL
The second brightest star in Perseus, Algol, nearly triples in brightness every three days. This is actually a pair of stars which revolve around each other every three days. When the stars are side-by-side, they are at their brightest. When the smallest star is in front, it eclipses, or covers, part of the larger star in the background causing the star to dim. Magnitude 2.1 to 3.4

PERSEUS DOUBLE CLUSTER
A pair of open clusters is located just above Perseus' head. It is quite unique to have two open clusters so close together. Both can be viewed within a single binocular view, though they are several hundred light years apart. Both are very distant at around 7,000 light years away! Magnitude 5.3

MYTHICAL HERO Perseus was a great hero in Greek mythology, and is recognized in the constellation story of Cassiopeia, Cepheus and Pegasus (see p. 30, 32 and 56), but his heroic adventures began long before he saved Andromeda. As a young man he was tricked by an evil king who promised to marry his mother unless he was able kill the dreaded Medusa, a gorgon whose hair was a mass of slithering snakes and whose stare turned people to stone. Two gods, Hermes and Athena, liked Perseus and guided him in his quest. Hermes, Zeus' messenger, gave him a sword and winged shoes that allowed him to fly. Athena gave him a shimmering shield and told him to use it as a mirror to look upon his victim without looking her in the eye. After a long journey, he found Medusa and her sisters. He looked into the mirror, saw his victim and cut off her head, then fled the scene. He returned with Medusa's head and freed his mother from captivity, before saving Andromeda from an equally scary monster. The hero was living large in his marriage with Andromeda. Unfortunately, before he was born, a prophecy had told that Perseus would kill his grandfather, a very important king. Perseus was ever-fearful of this prediction and swore that he would never kill a mortal man. One day, while practicing his discus throw, he released the disk a bit early and the misguided throw hit his grandfather right in the head, killing him instantly and making the prophecy true. Zeus commemorated the hero by placing him in the heavens.

Constellation Map

● **Perseus Double Cluster**
Two open star clusters
7,000 ly

Mirfak
Alpha star
593 ly

Algol
"The Demon Star"
Beta
93 ly

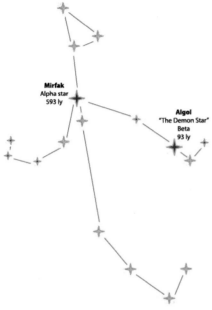

DISTANT STARS

Seventeen visible stars are connected together to make up Perseus' form. It is quite a large connect-the-dot game compared to most constellations. While Algol, the second brightest of the stars is "only" 93 light years away, the rest of the stars in this constellation are very distant. Three of the stars in this constellation are over 1,000 light years away.

THE DEMON STAR

Algol is commonly known as The Demon Star and represents Perseus' greatest trophy, the head of Medusa. As noted in the Fun Observations at left, this star is unique because its brightness varies dramatically from one night to the next. Be careful not to look too carefully, as those who look into her eyes might turn to stone!

Jesse Floria
7th grade

Sagittarius
The Archer

MONTHS IN THE SKY
July-October

OVERHEAD
Always low on the southern horizon

BRIGHTEST STAR
Kaus Australis (magnitude 1.8)

FIND IT
First, find Scorpius, an easy-to-find constellation low on the southern horizon (p. 62). Sagittarius is immediately next to the scorpion's tail.

FUN OBSERVATIONS

M8 LAGOON NEBULA
This cloud of hydrogen gas is over 100 light years wide (600 trillion miles!) and is a star factory. Astronomers estimate that over 1,000 new stars will be created from this gas. This cloud-like spot can be seen with the naked eye, but is better with binoculars. Magnitude 5

M20 TRIFID NEBULA
Another star factory, this one is best seen with a small telescope. It looks like three separate clouds, thus the name Trifid (*tri--* three), but it is one large hydrogen cloud. Magnitude 5

M23 OPEN CLUSTER
A big and bright open star cluster containing about 100 stars. Magnitude 6

M22 THE SAGITTARIUS CLUSTER
This globular cluster is a nursing home for dying stars. This cloud-like feature contains over half-a-million stars packed tightly and is 10,000 light years away! Magnitude 6.5

GREEK STORY Zeus' father was named Cronus. His own kids didn't like him much and were busy trying to overthrow the powerful Titan. For a time, Cronus hid himself by transforming into a horse. It makes sense that during these years of hiding he had a son named Chiron, who was born a centaur, half man and half horse. As Chiron grew up, he became an excellent archer and a master of medicine. His archery skills were so great, that many of the Greek warriors came to him to learn his techniques. Hercules, the mighty hunter who killed Leo the Lion and Draco the dragon, was studying under Chiron and stuck around one afternoon for a little extra target practice. As Chiron was walking back to his office at the end of the session, Hercules drew back his bow, became distracted and released a really bad shot. The arrow struck Chiron square in the back. Ouch! Being the son of a god, Chiron could not die, but he sure felt a lot of pain and the pain never went away, even for this medically trained centaur. The wound hurt so badly and for so long that he asked Zeus to let him die. Hercules convinced Zeus to let Chiron die, and in exchange, Prometheus could be released from the rock where he was chained and where Aquila, the eagle, nibbled away at his liver each day (p. 18). Chiron was honored for his great skill and sacrifice in the constellation Sagittarius.

Constellation Map

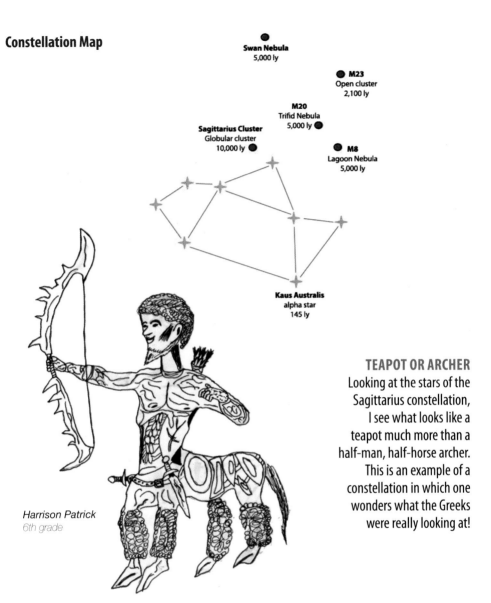

Swan Nebula
5,000 ly

M23
Open cluster
2,100 ly

M20
Trifid Nebula
5,000 ly

Sagittarius Cluster
Globular cluster
10,000 ly

M8
Lagoon Nebula
5,000 ly

Kaus Australis
alpha star
145 ly

Harrison Patrick
6th grade

TEAPOT OR ARCHER
Looking at the stars of the Sagittarius constellation, I see what looks like a teapot much more than a half-man, half-horse archer. This is an example of a constellation in which one wonders what the Greeks were really looking at!

LOOKING INTO THE MILKY WAY
Sagittarius is located in front of the cloudy backdrop of the Milky Way Galaxy. It is surrounded by so many sky features (see Constellation Map above) because of its location as we look toward the galaxy's center. The Milky Way is a flattened galaxy, shaped like a frisbee. Imagine that Earth is a fly that is embedded within the transparent plastic of the frisbee, near its outer edge. When we look up, down, left, right and most directions at all, we see randomly isolated stars that have been embedded nearby amidst a black background which is the open space beyond. But looking directly towards the center of the frisbee, and towards Sagittarius, we see a haze of plastic, or in this case the most dense collection of stars and other star stuff that make up the frisbee. The cloudy band that we see when looking into the Milky Way is just our view into the center of the galaxy.

family field guide

Scorpius
The Scorpion

MONTHS IN THE SKY
May-September

OVERHEAD
Remains low in the southern sky

BRIGHTEST STAR
Antares (magnitude 0.1)

FIND IT
Finding Antares, the brightest star in the scorpion, is the key to finding Scorpius. During the summer months, look low on the southern horizon and Antares is the brightest star out there. It has a reddish twinkle to it. To the right of Antares, three stars line up vertically to make the head. To the left, the tail hooks upward like a fishhook.

FUN OBSERVATIONS

M6 THE BUTTERFLY CLUSTER
This open cluster of new stars is estimated at 100 million years old. It is visible through binoculars and, through a telescope, the rough outline of a butterfly comes into view. Magnitude 4.5

M7 PTOLEMY CLUSTER
This open cluster is named after Claudius Ptolemy who recorded the first catalogue of 48 star constellations nearly 2,000 years ago. This very bright cluster is nearly visible with the naked eye on dark nights, and is clear through binoculars. Magnitude 3.5

GREEK MYTH Scorpius is part of the Orion myth. Orion the hunter lived on an island. He was a great hunter and owned two faithful hunting dogs (Canis Major and Canis Minor). Artemis, the goddess of the moon, drove her chariot across the sky every night, pulling the moon along behind her, and noticed the hunter on the deserted island. After watching him for many months, she decided to stop by for a visit, then another, and another until they fell in love. Needless to say, the moon's course was disrupted by these escapades and Zeus, god of the sky, was not happy at all. Rather than approaching Artemis in person, he sent a deadly scorpion down to the island to poison Orion in his sleep. Just as the Scorpion was about to attack, the hunting dogs growled and woke the hunter from his sleep. He immediately saw the enormous scorpion approaching and a battle ensued. They fought for hours. Just as Orion was in control of the situation, the moon began to rise. He looked over his shoulder to admire Artemis and her chariot. The scorpion squirmed loose and made a lethal attack. Orion died instantly. Artemis flew over the scene, saw what had happened and threw Orion into the sky as the great winter constellation and threw the scorpion into the sky as the low-lying summer constellation. She ensured that the two constellations were never in the sky at the same time, again.

Constellation Map

Antares
Alpha star
604 ly

M6
Butterfly Cluster
open cluster
2000 ly

M7
Ptolemy Cluster
open cluster
800 ly

M4
Cat's Eye Cluster
globular cluster
7,200 ly

GREEK NAME

Some folks misidentify Antares for Mars because both have such a red flare to them. While most stars have Arabic names, the Greeks claimed the naming rights for this red super giant and they, too, compared it to Mars. Mars is the Roman name for the Greek god, Ares. So, when the Greeks named it Antares they were comparing it to Ares, the God of War and his blood-red planet.

SOUTHERN VISITOR

Scorpius remains low on the southern horizon, just barely making its appearance in the Northern Hemisphere for a couple of months from mid to late summer. While it is a quick and low-lying visitor in the north, it is a prominent constellation in the Southern Hemisphere.

Chase Deneau
8th grade

ANTARES

Antares, the brightest star in the southern sky, is a red super giant. It is huge! It is among the brightest of stars in the sky and is much farther away than most magnitude 1 stars. While Sirius, the brightest star in the sky is only about 8 light years away, Antares is over 600 light years away. How could a star appear so bright from such an incredible distance? Because it is over 2,500 times larger than our sun!

Summer Triangle

MONTHS IN THE SKY
June-December

OVERHEAD
October

BRIGHTEST STAR
Vega (magnitude 0.0)

FIND IT
Look for the three brightest stars in the summer and autumn sky which form a very large triangle. Deneb and Altair are generally along the path of the Milky Way, while Vega is just to its side.

HISTORICAL NOTES
Arabic Language
Astronomer Claudius Ptolemy lived in Egypt. In 150 AD he published a book called the *Almagest*. This book named 48 star constellations and listed the names of over 1,000 stars. It was later printed in the Arabic language because astronomy was so important in Babylon and the Arabian Peninsula (modern day Saudi Arabia). This Arabic translation became more popular in Arabic than its original Latin text. The Arabic names of stars have continued to be the common names used by astronomers today. Examples of Arabic names in the Summer Triangle include Altair (the Flying Eagle) in Aquila, Deneb (Tail of the Hen) in Cygnus and Vega (The Stooping Eagle) in Lyra.

ASTERISM These three stars do not make up a constellation at all. The Summer Triangle is called an *asterism*; they are stars commonly connected in people's star gazing view, but do not form an official constellation. The first official list of 48 constellations, recorded nearly 2,000 years ago, did not include this giant triangle of bright stars. In 1930 the list was updated to include 88 official constellations. Again, the Summer Triangle did not make the list. Perhaps the Triangle is not an official constellation because the stars are spread quite far apart in the sky. Nonetheless, because these three stars are so bright, they create a good guidepost with which to navigate the summer sky.

APPARENT MAGNITUDE SCALE The Summer Triangle is easy to find because each of the three stars is of the first magnitude; they are among the brightest stars in the sky. The *apparent magnitude scale* is a system of classifying stars by their brightness; the brightest stars have a low magnitude and the numbers get larger as the stars get dimmer. This scale was devised over 2,000 years ago by a Greek astronomer named Hipparchus and is still used by scientists today! Hipparchus did not use a telescope or binoculars so his scale ranged from magnitude one to magnitude six. With the invention and improvement of telescopes, the scale has increased to include dim stars up to magnitude 30. The scale does not describe the amount of light produced by a star, only the brightness with which we see them.

Constellation Map

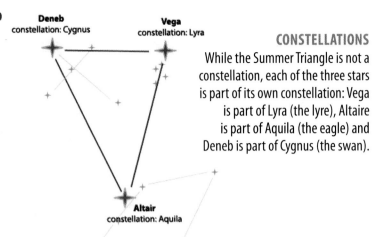

Deneb
constellation: Cygnus

Vega
constellation: Lyra

Altair
constellation: Aquila

CONSTELLATIONS

While the Summer Triangle is not a constellation, each of the three stars is part of its own constellation: Vega is part of Lyra (the lyre), Altaire is part of Aquila (the eagle) and Deneb is part of Cygnus (the swan).

ALTAIRE

At 17 light years away, Altair is the closest of the Summer Triangle stars and is recognized as the fastest of the stars in the triangle. All stars spin around an axis in the same way that the earth rotates around its axis every 24 hours. Our sun completes one rotation each month and Altaire requires only 6.5 hours. This super-fast spin affects the shape of the star. Imagine spinning really fast on an amusement park ride; your hair pulls back and your body is pushed back and rides are equipped with heavy duty seat belts so that you don't fly out of the ride. The same thing is happening with Altaire. Its rapid spin is pushing its body outward, giving it a short, squatty shape. Scientists estimate that it is only half as tall as it is wide thanks to the force created by its extreme rotation.

DENEB

At 1,500 light years away, this red giant is the most distant and the largest star in the Summer Triangle. While Deneb appears similarly as bright as Vega and Altair, it is nearly 100 times farther away than Vega. The light that we see was created on the star's surface before the Anasazi indians moved into Mesa Verde. It has been traveling through space ever since and is now arriving in your eyesight! Even at this distance, it is one of the brightest stars in the night sky. That is because it is equal to 200 of our suns combined and shines 300,000 times brighter.

VEGA

Vega is the brightest star in the Summer Triangle and is the second brightest star in the summer sky, after Arcturus. Using some serious mathematical calculations, scientists estimate that Vega was the pole star in 12,000 BC and it will be again in 13,000 AD.

Taurus
The Bull

MONTHS IN THE SKY
November-April

OVERHEAD
February

BRIGHTEST STAR
Aldebaran (magnitude 0.9)

FIND IT
First locate Orion. Extend a nearly-straight line upward from Orion's Belt to the brightest red star. This is Aldebaran, the brightest star in Taurus. Aldebaran is one of the 4 stars that form a small Y. The tips of the Y extend nearly two fist lengths outward.

FUN OBSERVATIONS

PLAEIDES STAR CLUSTER
Perhaps the most famous star cluster in the sky, the Plaeides is a group of newly formed stars, all formed from the same mass of gases. It is the brightest *star cluster* in the sky and is only 410 ly away. Because it is brighter than some constellations (Delphinus for example), it is sometimes mistaken as its own constellation.
Magnitude 1.4

HYADES STAR CLUSTER
This open star cluster is directly behind Aldebaran, the brightest star in Taurus. These 40-50 stars are quite old and are spread out so much that they are hardly noticeable as a cluster. While the Plaeides is the brightest star cluster in the sky, the Hyades is the closest at only 150 light years distant. Though Aldebaran and the Hyades align visually, the red giant is not related to these young stars.
Magnitude .5

A GOD'S TRICK Zeus loved women. He looked at them, fell in love with them, dreamed about them and those who would not accept him were the women he dreamed about the most. Though he was married, he noticed a beautiful woman named Europa and, for a while, she was the girl of his dreams. He used all of his best lines to woo her into his love grasp, but nothing he did was charming enough to catch Europa's attention. Zeus knew that she raised prize bulls and that she had an eye for impressive livestock. He disguised himself as a bull and went walking among her pastures. She noticed him right away and befriended the new bull. Within weeks he became her favorite. After many hours of grooming, she felt comfortable enough to saddle up on the hulking beast at which point the bull took off running with her on his back. He ran all the way across the country, through the ocean and onto an island where she couldn't escape his affection. Finally he revealed his true identity and she didn't mind the trick one bit. As was the way with Zeus, even though he'd won the love of the woman he wanted, he started looking at other women again. In the end, she dumped the cheating god. While their story isn't one of life-long love, Zeus remembered the good ride and put the bull in the stars. While the Greeks remembered the bull in this constellation, Europa was later memorialized by name as one of the four moons that revolves around Jupiter.

Constellation Map

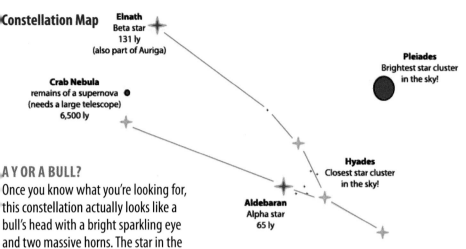

Elnath
Beta star
131 ly
(also part of Auriga)

Crab Nebula
remains of a supernova
(needs a large telescope)
6,500 ly

Pleiades
Brightest star cluster
in the sky!

Hyades
Closest star cluster
in the sky!

Aldebaran
Alpha star
65 ly

A Y OR A BULL?

Once you know what you're looking for, this constellation actually looks like a bull's head with a bright sparkling eye and two massive horns. The star in the middle, where the forks meet, is the bull's muzzle. Moving up the forks, the two stars that are side by side are the eyes, one of which is Aldebaran, the brightest star in the constellation. The continuing fork represents the bull's horns.

SUPERNOVA

The Crab Nebula (see map above) was the first observation recorded by Charles Messier. This burst of light is the continued motion of a *supernova*, an exploding star. The star exploded in 1054 and was so bright that it was visible in the daytime for nearly a month. Ancient astronomers recorded that it was visible to the naked eye for many years after it exploded. The Anasazi indians carved a pictograph that records this *supernova* event in Chaco Canyon (New Mexico). A similar record was discovered in China, also dating back to 1054. Today a medium telescope is needed to see the fading blast.

Mariel Gorsuch
5th grade

PLAEIDES

Though is is commonly called The Seven Sisters, only six of the stars in this open cluster are visible to the naked eye today. Some guess that one of the stars has burned out or dimmed since ancient times. In Japanese, this cluster is called Subaru and is the namesake for the car company. Their symbol is a cluster of six stars which represents this nighttime sky feature. It is so bright and obvious that it can be used as the guidepost to help find Taurus.

Ursa Major
The Great Bear

MONTHS IN THE SKY
Year-round (at latitudes north of 40 degrees)

OVERHEAD
May

BRIGHTEST STAR
Alioth (magnitude 1.7)

FIND IT
The key to this constellation is the Big Dipper. The Dipper is the hind quarters and tail of the the Big Bear. Use the constellation map to piece together the rest of this large constellation.

FUN OBSERVATIONS
MIZAR AND ALCOR
The second star from the end of the handle is actually a pair of stars that can be seen with the naked eye in dark skies.
Magnitude 2.2 and 4

HISTORICAL NOTES
Big Horn Medicine Wheel
Constructed 300-800 years ago in modern-day Wyoming, this stone structure is at the top of a 10,000 foot mountain. Twenty-eight spokes extend from a central point which may have marked the days in the lunar cycle. Many believe that the layout of this structure records the rising and setting sun on the summer solstice. Stones within the wheel may have marked the rising of the bright stars Aldebaran, Rigel and Sirius.

GREEK TRAGEDY Zeus was the king of the gods and is known for his love affairs with many women. Naturally, his wife Hera was very jealous and often took revenge against these other women. Such is the case in the story of the bears. A single mother named Callisto was washing her laundry at a stream when Zeus walked by. He flashed his godly smile and caught the attention of the innocent lady. She fell for his kind greeting and they went out for a walk together. Hera saw them walking arm-in-arm and she lost it. She pointed her finger at Callisto and turned her into a great bear. Callisto the bear wandered the forest for months, leaving her only son, Arcus, to fend for himself. Fortunately, he was a skilled hunter so he never had to go hungry. One day, he was out with his bow and arrows, sneaking through the forest when he spotted a great bear. Of course he did not recognize the bear as his mother, so he drew back his bow and steadied himself, ready to plug her right in the heart. Fortunately, Zeus jumped into the scene and interrupted the boy, telling him not to shoot. He was so hungry and loved the hunt so much, even a god couldn't distract him. Arcus didn't drop the bow and was about to release the arrow when Zeus made the split second decision to save Callisto by turning her son, Arcus, into a bear. He grabbed both bears by the tails and swung them up into the sky where they circle the northern sky, one Great Bear and one Little Bear, side by side. Callisto was later memorialized by name as one of the four moons that revolves around Jupiter.

Constellation Map

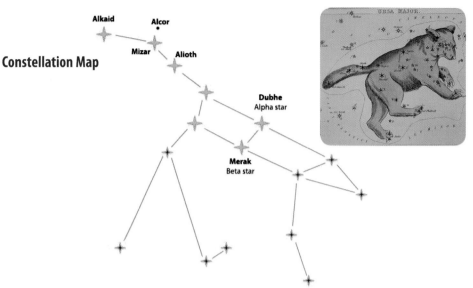

Alkaid

Alcor

Mizar Alioth

Dubhe
Alpha star

Merak
Beta star

NATIVE AMERICAN MYTH

The Iroquois tribe of North America refers to the three stars in the Dipper's handle, Alioth, Mizar and Alkaid, as three hunters who follow the Great Bear in their hunt. The second hunter, Mizar, carries a pot to cook the bear following their successful hunt. The pot is the very faint star, Alcor, just above Mizar, which is barely visible with the naked eye. The Algonquin, Illinois and Narragansett tribes of North America also envisioned a bear in these stars.

Gabe Hjorth
8th grade

BIG CONSTELLATION

The Big Dipper is the most commonly recognized of all star groups, though it is only a part of this bigger constellation. The Big Dipper makes up only about 1/3 of this constellation, the third largest of all the constellations in the sky.

Ursa Minor
The Little Bear

MONTHS IN THE SKY
Year-round (at latitudes north of 40 degrees)

OVERHEAD
May

BRIGHTEST STAR
Polaris/The North Star (magnitude 2.0)

FIND IT
Finding Polaris is the key to this constellation. First locate the two stars that make up the end of the Big Dipper's cup. Extend a nearly-straight line as those two stars pour out of the Dipper three fist-lengths to the brightest star in the area, the North Star (see p. 25). Use the Constellation Map to find the rest of this tricky constellation.

HISTORICAL NOTES
Stonehenge (2500 BC)
This rock structure, built on the rolling plains of England, holds more questions than answers. Many scientists believe that it was some sort of observatory. Many of its features line up nearly to solstices, equinoxes and the rising of stars, but nothing matches up as precisely as structures built by Egyptians, Mayans and others. The purpose of this monument remains unknown, but many believe that it was somehow built to honor and record movements of the sun, moon and stars.

GREEK TRAGEDY For a full descripiton of this Greek story refer to p. 66. In summary, Zeus' wife Hera had turned a lovely young lady into a bear. While the big bear roamed the forest, her human son was left an orphan to fend for himself. The son was out hunting for food one day and was about to shoot the big bear, not knowing that it was his mother. Zeus entered the scene and demanded that the boy put down his arrow. The hungry child ignored the god and was about to shoot. In an effort to save the big bear, Zeus turned the boy into a little bear so that the mother and son could be reunited. He placed the the big bear, Ursa Major, and the little bear, Ursa Minor, together in the sky.

APPARENT MAGNITUDE TEST Ursa Minor is a good tool to better understand the *Apparent Magnitude Scale* (p. 10). The North Star is the brightest star in Ursa Minor and has an apparent magnitude of 2. Other stars in the constellation have a magnitude of 3, 4 and 5 (see Constellation Map at right). Ursa Minor provides a good comparison of the brightness of stars and their relationship to the Apparent Magnitude Scale.

TAILS AND HANDLES As we know them, bears don't have long tails, but when Zeus threw these bears up into the sky, their tails stretched out like a mountain lion's. As for the Little Dipper, it's harder to identify than the Big Dipper because the handle is either bent really badly or it is connected to the bottom part of the dipper. Either way it is a very tippy dipper and is tricky to identify.

family field guide

Constellation Map

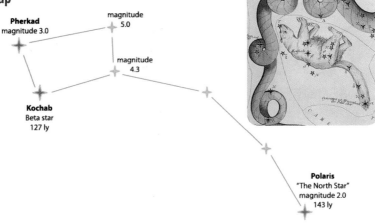

Pherkad
magnitude 3.0

magnitude 5.0

magnitude 4.3

Kochab
Beta star
127 ly

Polaris
"The North Star"
magnitude 2.0
143 ly

POLE STARS

It is unique that the Northern Hemisphere has a star that lines directly with Earth's axis. At present, no star lines up with Earth's axis in the Southern Hemisphere, so there is no southern pole star.

THE NORTH STAR

The brightest star of Ursa Minor (The Little Dipper) is the most important star in the sky, not because of its brightness, but because of its location. The North Star has been used as a navigational tool for as long as people have been looking at the stars. All of the stars in the sky rotate throughout the night and throughout the seasons, except for one: the North Star. Because it does not move, sailors, explorers and escapees have forever used the North Star as a compass point. Once the North Star is identified, it is easy to find the cardinal directions. With a little more math and science knowledge, advanced explorers can pinpoint their exact latitude and longitude.

Virgo
The Virgin

MONTHS IN THE SKY
March-August

OVERHEAD
May

BRIGHTEST STAR
Spica (magnitude 1.0)

FIND IT
Finding Spica, the brightest star in Virgo, is the key to locating this constellation. Follow the arc of the Big Dipper's handle three fist-lengths to the brightest star, Arcturus (constellation Bootes). Next, spike downward another three fist-lengths to the next brightest star, Spica. Remember the saying, "Follow the arc to Arcturus, then spike down to Spica." Use the constellation map to find the rest of Virgo.

FUN OBSERVATIONS
VIRGO CLUSTER
Located in the upper right corner of the Virgo constellation is a collection of nearly 2,000 different galaxies. Most of these are only visible with high-powered telescopes, but sixteen of them were recorded by Charles Messier in 1781. Galaxies weren't even understood until the 1920s! Consider that the earth and its planets are enormous on a human scale and that our single galaxy, The Milky Way, is larger than most people can even comprehend. Within this single part of the sky, there are over 2,000 galaxies, each with billions of stars and planets and gravitational forces and who-knows-what-else.

MYTHOLOGY These stars have been consistently related to powerful women and their ability to grow and nurture throughout a broad range of cultures. In India, these stars are related to Kauni, mother of the god Krishna. The ancient Babylonians (near modern-day Iraq) associated these stars with the goddess Ishtar. She went down to the underworld to get her husband, the god of the harvest, and the earth went dark and nothing grew. When she returned to the world with her husband, the earth blossomed again. Later, in Greek mythology, Persephone, daughter of Zeus and Demeter, was kidnapped and taken to the underworld. Her mom was so angry that she destroyed the harvest and many people starved. Zeus talked with his brother, the ruler of the underworld, and they came to a compromise. Persephone would only spend half of each year among the living world and half of each year in the underworld. Her mother, Demeter, was not entirely satisfied with the deal and in return, promised to allow the earth to blossom when her daughter was among the living and she would make it all die during the time when her daughter was taken away. Virgo represents the annual trip to the underworld which brings the onset of winter, and the return to the living, and the onset of spring.

ZODIAC The sun's path crosses through Virgo from September 17-October 30. Because the sun aligns with Virgo during the harvest season, this constellation has been associated with farming and the seasons.

family field guide

Constellation Map

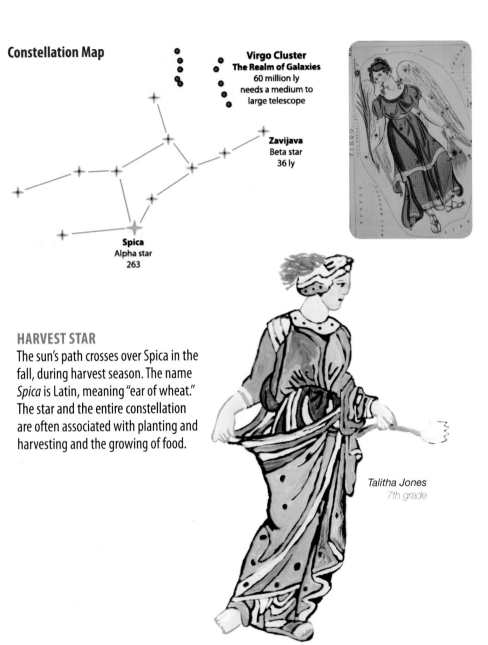

Virgo Cluster
The Realm of Galaxies
60 million ly
needs a medium to
large telescope

Zavijava
Beta star
36 ly

Spica
Alpha star
263

HARVEST STAR

The sun's path crosses over Spica in the fall, during harvest season. The name *Spica* is Latin, meaning "ear of wheat." The star and the entire constellation are often associated with planting and harvesting and the growing of food.

Talitha Jones
7th grade

SPICA

The brightest star in Virgo is 275 light years away. The light which leaves the star today will finally be visible nine generations from now. Even at this distance, it is among the brightest stars in the sky which means it must be an enormous and very bright star; it is nearly 2,000 times brighter than our sun! Spica has a companion star which orbits around it every four days. The companion is 11 million miles distant from Spica and produces about 20% of the brightness that we see. They are close enough together that we cannot see the separation, except with a high-powered telescope.

family field guide

Planets
The Wanderers

HISTORICAL NOTES
Hipparchus (190 BC-120 BC)

This Greek astronomer is recognized as the greatest observer of astronomy in ancient times. His writings and drawings recorded the movements of the sun, moon, stars and planets in great detail. While similar observations occurred around the world in the same time period, most were recorded in rock art by native tribes. Hipparchus, on the other hand, recorded volumes of detailed sketches and descriptions of the universe. He formulated different orbiting patterns and was the first to predict solar and lunar eclipses using math as his proof. He recorded the first catalogue of the stars in the Northern Hemisphere and created the Apparent Magnitude Scale to describe the brightness of stars.

WHAT IS A PLANET? A planet is any large ball of rock, gas or metal that revolves around a star. Within our solar system, eight planets revolve around our sun. Scientists have found hundreds of other planets in the universe that revolve around stars of their own. Planets do not give off their own light. In the case of our neighboring planets, we see the light of the sun reflecting off of their surface. Our neighboring planets appear very bright in our sky simply because they are much closer to Earth than the stars.

WANDERERS The word *planet* comes from a Greek word meaning "wanderer." Early astronomers from many different cultures realized that the planets were different from the stars. While stars follow a similar pattern every night and every year, these random lights appear in the sky on a totally different schedule from the stars. They were considered wanderers in the night sky. Many cultures thought of these wandering lights as visitors of the gods or other spiritual messengers and they received great attention and appreciation.

TYPES OF PLANETS There are two types of planets in our solar system. Those with a rocky surface are called *terrestrial* planets and the *gas giants*, or *Jovian planets*, are gassy balls held together by gravity. The planets nearest the sun are all terrestrial planets (Mercury, Venus, Earth and Mars) and the more distant planets are gas giants (Jupiter, Saturn, Uranus and Neptune).

family field guide

A SOLAR SYSTEM

A solar system is any series of planets that revolve around a star. *Solar* is another word for "sun" and *system* refers to many things working together. Scientists have found at least 500 other planets out there in space that revolve around stars, so there are many solar systems quite similar to our own.

FIVE VISIBLE PLANETS

Of the eight planets in our solar system, only five are visible with the naked eye or binoculars. Venus and Mercury are visible in mornings and evenings. Mars, Jupiter and Saturn can all be seen throughout the night. The planets appear in our sky at varying times based on their orbiting patterns.

Jaclyn Harris
6th grade

WHAT HAPPENED TO PLUTO?

For over 75 years scientists recognized nine planets in our solar system. That all changed in 2006 when Pluto lost its claim as the smallest and most distant planet in our solar system. Pluto is a round, rocky ball of ice and rock that revolves around the sun along with many other large, icy objects in a band called the Kuiper Belt. In 2003, scientists found several objects of equal size to Pluto, and one that is quite a bit larger, all orbiting the sun within the Kuiper Belt. In August of 2006, astronomers decided that because Pluto doesn't have its own, unique orbit, it is not a planet. They now call it a dwarf planet, so there are only eight official planets in our solar system.

Jupiter

DIAMETER
88,844 miles (11 times larger than Earth)

LENGTH OF DAY (One full rotation)
9.8 hours

LENGTH OF YEAR (One orbit around sun)
11.8 Earth years

AVERAGE TEMPERATURE
-162° F

HISTORICAL NOTES

Claudius Ptolemy (90-168)
Ptolemy was a French-born astronomer who lived most of his life in Egypt almost 2,000 years ago. He published a book called *The Almagest* in 150 AD which became the most commonly used star guide for hundreds of years. Much of the information in his book was gathered by the Greeks, so he is not the discoverer of so many things, but his collection of work was used by so many people and for so many years that his lists of constellations and thousands of star names became the standard astronomy language around much of Europe and the Arabic world.

BIG, BIGGER, BIGGEST Jupiter is by far the biggest planet in our solar system. It is more than twice the size of all the other planets combined. Over 1,300 Earths could fit into the space of this gassy planet. While it is one of the most distant of the visible planets, it appears brighter than any of the stars in the sky because of its size. Sirius, the brightest star, has a magnitude of -1.4 while Jupiter's measures a brighter -2.7 (remember, the lower the number, the brighter the light).

THE GREAT RED SPOT The most distinguishing feature of Jupiter is the Great Red Spot (GRS) located on the lower right side of Jupiter in the above picture. The GRS appears as a red oval shape on the surface of Jupiter. It is actually a cool area where the clouds rise much higher than than those on the rest of the planet. This constant storm is larger than two Earths combined! The GRS was first documented over 300 years ago and can be seen with a small telescope. Because Jupiter is spinning, the GRS is not always facing towards Earth.

GASSY GIANT Though Jupiter is huge, its center core is quite small. That core, though, is surrounded by layers and layers of gas. Hydrogen is the most common gas in space and Helium is the next most abundant. It is no surprise that Jupiter is 90% Hydrogen and 10% Helium. This combination of gases is similar to most stars, but unlike the stars, Jupiter is not nearly large enough to begin *nuclear fusion*, the process that ignites into a fiery star.

Viewing Dates of Jupiter

Date of Opposition*	Minimum Distance from Earth	Best Viewing
10/27/2011	369 million miles	Sept. 2011 to Dec. 2011
12/1/2012	378 million miles	Oct. 2012 to Jan. 2013
1/4/2014	392 million miles	Dec. 2013 to March 2014
2/4/2015	404 million miles	Dec. 2014 to April 2015
3/8/2016	412 million miles	Jan. 2016 to May 2016

Opposition occurs when Earth is directly between Jupiter and the sun.

MYTH BUSTER
Boys do not go to Jupiter to get much stupider. It's just not true.

NAME
The largest planet in our solar system is named after the Roman god Jupiter. The Romans left a great mark on civilization, but they weren't entirely original when it came to creating their gods. They borrowed the ideas of the Greek gods, then changed the names to make them their own. Jupiter was the king of the Roman gods, the equivalent of Zeus in the Greek tradition. Like Zeus, Jupiter was the king of the sky and controlled thunder, lightning and the law.

Talitha Jones
7th grade

JUPITER'S MOONS
Four visible moons revolve around Jupiter and are easily seen through binoculars. Four hundred years ago, in 1610, astronomer Galileo Galilei used his telescope to observe Jupiter's moons. Each time he looked, they were in different locations. He concluded that the moons were revolving around the planet. This observation, that objects in space revolve around things not of this earth, supported the possibility that Earth might possibly rotate around the sun, a shocking idea in that time. His observations of Jupiter's moons earned them the name: *The Galilean Satellites*. Their individual names are Callisto, Io, Europa and Ganemede, commemorating several of Zeus' mistresses. Callisto is also remembered in Ursa Major and Europa in Taurus.

Mars

DIAMETER
4,222 miles (half the size of Earth)

LENGTH OF DAY (one full rotation)
24.6 hours

LENGTH OF YEAR (one orbit around sun)
687 Earth years

AVERAGE TEMPERATURE
-81° F

HISTORICAL NOTES
Nicolaus Copernicus (1473-1543)
In the centuries leading up to Copernicus' life, the Western world believed that the earth was the center of the universe. They believed the sun, the stars, the planets and the moon all revolved around the earth. Copernicus was the first person to suggest that the sun was the center of our solar system. He called his idea the *heliocentric model* (*helio*-sun; *centric*-center). He was a mathematician by profession, astronomy was more of a hobby, and his idea was not accepted in his lifetime. He died shortly after publishing his model, but his revolutionary idea sparked the possibility for future astronomers to find further evidence to support his theory, that the earth was not the center of the universe.

SIMILARITIES While Venus is known as Earth's sister planet because of their similar sizes, Mars has more features similar to Earth's composition. It is a rocky planet, it has a similar tilt as Earth's axis which gives it varying seasons and changing weather, it has a similar day-length and, most interesting, there is evidence of water. These features have made it an interesting test subject for scientists. While it is similar to Earth, it has several conditions that do not allow people to survive there. It is a frozen desert that is colder than a chilly Antarctic afternoon in winter, and, more importantly, it has an atmosphere that is mostly Carbon Dioxide (we humans prefer to inhale Oxygen). Still, many scientists believe that astronauts will walk on Mars within the next 30 years or so.

ADVENTURER'S PARADISE Mars has some interesting landforms on its surface. An inactive volcano towers 15 miles above the surface, three times taller than Mt. Everst. A canyon is gouged into the surface that is four miles deep, four times deeper than the Grand Canyon. Talk about an adventurer's dreamland! A billion or so years ago, Mars might have had oceans and rivers which created some of the features on Mars' surface. This evidence of water has scientists carefully looking for the presence of past life.

MYTH BUSTER To the disbelief of many young girls, there are no candy bars on Mars.

family field guide

Viewing Dates of Mars

Date of Opposition*	Minimum Distance from Earth	Best Viewing
3/3/2012	62.3 million miles	Feb. 2012 to May 2012
4/8/2014	58 million miles	March 2014 to June 2014
5/22/2016	47.3 million miles	April 2016 to July 2016
7/27/2018	35.8 million miles	June 2018 to Sept. 2018
1/13/2020	38.5 million miles	Dec. 2019 to March 2020

*Opposition occurs when Earth is directly between Mars and the sun.

ORBIT

As Earth and Mars move along their orbits, Earth passes directly between the sun and Mars every 26 months. This is called its *opposition*. Because of their oval-shaped orbits, the planets pass by each other at varying distances in each cycle. Mathematicians use the shape and speed of these orbits to predict the movements of the planets. Mars made its closest pass to Earth in 2003 (35 million miles away) and will do it again in 2050, then again in 2082. Mark these on your calendar so you can watch with your kids and grandkids!

NAMES

Mars is the Roman god of war, comparable to the Greek god, Ares. The Romans may have named it after their god of war because of its blood-red color. The planet is also commonly called *The Red Planet* because it shines red in the night sky. The surface of the planet is covered with a layer of fine, red dust. There is a lot of iron in the dust, which gives it the red color and probably originated from volcanic eruptions that pushed magma, with high concentrations of iron, to the surface. Below the dust layer, Mars is dull grey, but the surface dust creates a red color when reflected by the sun.

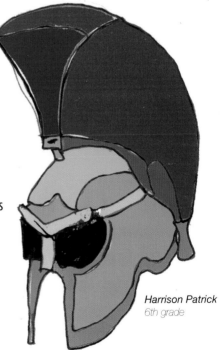

Harrison Patrick
6th grade

MARS ROVERS

Two remote-controlled golf-carts (called rovers) named *Opportunity* and *Spirit*, were sent to Mars in 2004 to take pictures of the planet and to collect rock, dust and other samples. These high-tech robots have given scientists new and interesting information about the planet's geography, geology, hydrology, weather and other features.

Mercury

DIAMETER
3,032 miles (less than half of Earth)

LENGTH OF DAY (one full rotation)
30 earth days

LENGTH OF YEAR (one orbit around sun)
88 Earth days

TEMPERATURE RANGE
-290° F-800° F

HISTORICAL NOTES
Galileo (1564-1642)

Galileo Galilei is known as the "father of modern observational astronomy." Though the first telescope was invented in 1608 by a Dutch astronomer, Hans Lippershey, Galileo made the telescope a practical and useful tool by the year 1610. This tool allowed him to make many new discoveries. Most notably, he was the first to observe the moons orbiting Jupiter, which are now known as the Galilean Satellites. As he observed these moons orbiting their mother planet, he concluded that the Earth might, in fact, orbit the sun, an idea that was not accepted at the time. Because of his observations, his volumes of records and use of scientific observation, Albert Einstein called him, "The father of modern science."

MORNING STAR, EVENING STAR Because Mercury is loated between the earth and the sun, it is only visible very near to the sun. For this reason, Mercury and Venus, the other inner planets, are only visible near the sun just before sunrise and just after sunset. Mercury travels high in the sky during the day when the sky is too bright to see it.

HOT, COLD AND NASTY Mercury is an uncomfortable planet. Like Earth, it spins on its axis, but because it is so close to the sun, the side that is facing the sun is exposed to extreme heat. Also, its rotation is much slower than Earth's, an entire month is required to complete a single rotation, so the side of the planet that is opposite the sun remains shaded for a long time and gets very cold. Besides these temperature extremes, the air surrounding Mercury's surface is mostly Nitrogen; there isn't any Oxygen around Mercury at all, not even in the form of Carbon Dioxide.

CRATERS Mercury looks similar to our moon. It is gray in color and has thousands of craters from space-rocks that have crashed into its surface. These rocks are constantly hurling through space. When the meteoroids approach Earth, they burn up in our atmosphere (we see these as "shooting stars"), but Mercury does not have much of an atmosphere to protect it, so it is easily bombarded, creating a cratered surface.

family field guide

Viewing Dates of Mercury

Best Viewing	Time	Best Viewing	Time
Mid-November 2011	Evening	Late March 2013	Morning
Mid-December 2011	Morning	Early June 2013	Evening
Early March 2012	Evening	Early August 2013	Morning
Mid-April 2012	Morning	Early October 2013	Evening
Late June 2012	Evening	Mid-November 2013	Morning
Mid-August 2012	Morning	Late Jan-Early Feb. 2014	Evening
Late October 2012	Evening	Late Feb.-Early March 2014	Morning
Early December 2012	Morning	Late May 2014	Evening
Mid-February 2013	Evening	Mid-July 2014	Morning

VIEWING MERCURY

Mercury has a very *eliptical,* or oval-shaped, orbit so its distance from the earth and the sun varies tremendously. Because of this huge variation, its *apparent magnitude* ranges from a very bright -2.3 to a very dim, and hardly visible, 5.7. It comes into view much more frequently than any of the other planets, but it only stays in the sky for a couple weeks at a time. These frequent, short-lived visits are due to its quick orbit around the sun.

PROBES

Mercury is difficult to study because of its extreme temperatures and its toxic air. Scientists have sent unmanned spacecrafts, called *probes,* near Mercury which have taken pictures of the surface and measurements of the surrounding air. Even though no human could ever go to Mercury, these probes allow us to understand a bit of its environment.

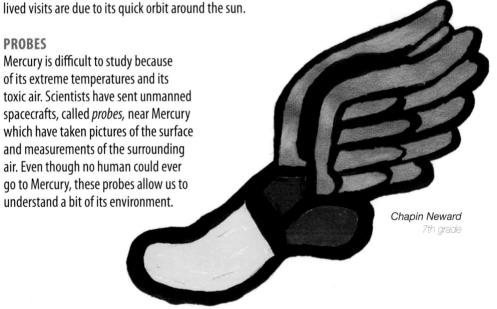

Chapin Neward
7th grade

NAME Because it is only visible at dawn and dusk and it appears in different parts of the sky, in the east at dawn and in the west at dusk, early astronomers thought they were seeing two different planets. The Greeks named one of the planets Apollo and the other Hermes. Later, the Romans recognized it as one planet and they applied the name Mercury, the equivalent of the Greek god Hermes, the messenger who used his winged shoes to run quickly from place to place. Similar to the messenger god, Mercury is the fastest orbiting planet; its appearances in the sky are frequent, but only last a few weeks before disappearing again.

family field guide

Saturn

DIAMETER
74,900 miles (10 times larger than Earth)

LENGTH OF DAY (one full rotation)
10.2 hours

LENGTH OF YEAR (one orbit around sun)
29 Earth years

AVERAGE TEMPERATURE
-218° F

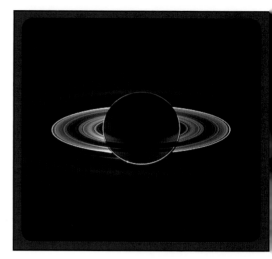

HISTORICAL NOTES
Isaac Newton (1643-1772)
Newton combined his observations of the natural world with mathematics to help shape scientific understanding. In 1668, sixty years after Galileo's telescope, Newton placed a mirror between the lenses to create a much clearer and more accurate magnified view. His telescope was called a *reflecting telescope* and is the basis for many modern-day telescopes. He also had mathematical proof of gravitational forces and motion which explained how the earth and other objects could hold their orbiting patterns around other larger objects. His mathematical explanations proved to the remaining doubters that the earth could revolve around the sun, thus proving, once and for all, that Copernicus and Galileos' theories were correct.

RINGS Saturn is the favorite planet of most young sky watchers because of its rings. It is not the only planet with rings, but its rings are easily visible with a small telescope. Early astronomer and creator of the first functional telescope, Galileo Gelilei, first observed Saturn's rings in 1610, four hundred years ago. For centuries people thought the rings were solid, but newer technology has revealed that they are bits of rock and dust hurling through space in an orbit around the planet. Most of the rocks are small, about the size of a Coke can, but some may be a mile or so in diameter.

MOON PARTICLES Scientists and curious kids have long wondered why Saturn has such unique rings. The leading theory is that a moon once orbited the gassy planet, but it was smashed to pieces by an asteroid or other large object. As it exploded, all of the particles continued to orbit Saturn, and they never rejoined as a single mass again. Instead, they continued to smash into each other, breaking into smaller and smaller pieces as they continued to orbit as the original moon once did.

GASSY PLANET Saturn is a huge ball of gas. It is so far away that scientists haven't studied it in detail, but they imagine that there is a solid core in its center. That core, though, must be pretty small since Saturn is the least dense of any of the planets. If you could build an enormous bathtub and give Saturn a good washing, it would float because those gases, all pooled together, are less dense than water.

family field guide

Viewing Dates of Saturn

Date of Opposition*	Minimum Distance from Earth	Best Viewing
4/3/2011	801 million miles	March 2011 to July 2011
4/15/2012	811 million miles	Mid-March 2012 to mid-July 2012
4/27/2013	820 million miles	Late March 2013 to late July 2013
5/9/2014	828 million miles	April 2014 to July 2014
5/23/2015	837 million miles	Late April 2015 to August 2015
6/3/2016	837 million miles	May 2016 to August 2016

*Opposition occurs when Earth is directly between Saturn and the sun.

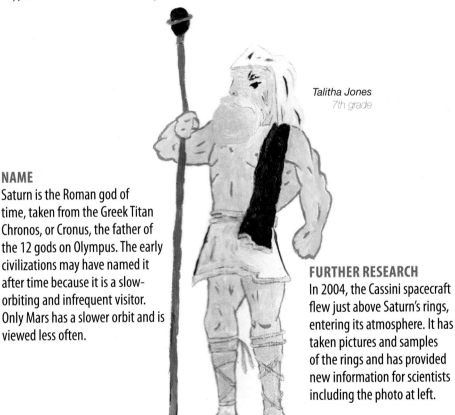

Talitha Jones
7th grade

NAME

Saturn is the Roman god of time, taken from the Greek Titan Chronos, or Cronus, the father of the 12 gods on Olympus. The early civilizations may have named it after time because it is a slow-orbiting and infrequent visitor. Only Mars has a slower orbit and is viewed less often.

FURTHER RESEARCH

In 2004, the Cassini spacecraft flew just above Saturn's rings, entering its atmosphere. It has taken pictures and samples of the rings and has provided new information for scientists including the photo at left.

VIEWING

Saturn is one of the most enjoyable planets to see because its rings are so unique. The rings cannot be seen through binoculars, but a small telescope brings them into view. When looking at Saturn, we see it from varying angles in each orbiting cycle. Some years we see it tilted and the rings are very obvious. Other years we view it straight on and cannot see the rings at all. The rings are only as thick as a football field, and looking at them when they are directly horizontal is like looking at the cross-section of a Kleenex.

Sun

DIAMETER
865,278 miles (100 times bigger than Earth)

AGE
4.6 billion years

NUMBER OF PLANETS
8 planets, 3 dwarf planets

CORE TEMPERATURE
27,000,000° F

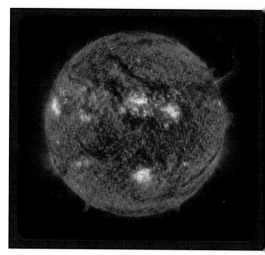

HISTORICAL NOTES
Charles Messier (1730-1817)

Messier was a French-born astronomer and an avid comet hunter. As he scoured the night sky for moving light objects (comets), he kept detailed records of every little light object he observed. He described them by number, adding his initial, M, before each one. Most of the sky features that he observed did not move, proving that they were not comets, but in his process he recorded more deep sky objects than any other astronomer in history. In all, he observed 103 different galaxies, open star clusters, globular clusters and nebulae and he catalogued them accordingly, M1-M103. After his death, astronomers found evidence of seven other objects that were noted by Messier, but not officially recorded, and they gave him credit, so his catalogue actually includes M1-M110.

STARS Our sun is a star, just like any other. A huge mass of burning Hydrogen, it does not have a solid core. Stars do not burn in the way that we burn wood or coal; no match was needed to start their fire. Instead, the Hydrogen molecules ram together so tight and fast that they join together or fuse. This process is called *nuclear fusion* and it is constantly happening, creating tremendous amounts of heat and light.

LIFESPAN Our sun has been burning for nearly 5 billion years. Eventually, it will start to run out of Hydrogen, the source of its fire. As this happens, it will begin to swell bigger and bigger until it becomes a red giant. It will grow large enough to swallow up the first four planets, but don't worry, that won't happen for another 5 billion years or so. After it swells outward and burns the final little bits of Hydrogen, it will shrink again into a very dense ball of fire and become a measly *white dwarf* star.

SOURCE OF LIFE The sun is the source of life on this planet. It provides us with just enough heat that life can thrive, but not so much that we fry like bacon. It also gives us just enough light that plants can convert its light energy into food energy, so that they can grow...and be eaten. In that sense, we are eating the sun's energy. When we light up a campfire, we are burning the sun's rays stored in the tree's wood. All of the energy that moves through our environment is solar energy in different forms.

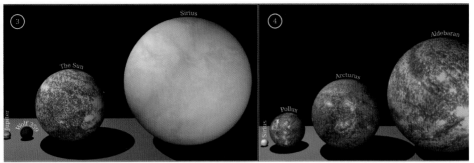

Our sun is much bigger than the largest planet Jupiter as seen in picture 3, but it is much, much smaller than other giant stars as shown compared to Sirius in picture 4.

SUN GODS

Throughout history, people have celebrated the sun. The Egyptians had a variety of sun gods, including Isis, who were rowed across the sky in boats and, later, in chariots. The Aztecs had a variety of sun gods who guarded heaven. The Greeks celebrated Apollo as the god of the sun. Celebrations have forever occurred around the Northern Hemisphere on the summer solstice which marks the longest day of the year, when the sun is highest in the sky and pays its longest daily visit to Earth.

Sarah Elice
7th grade

SEASONS

The sun travels on a predictable path throughout the year. In the Northern Hemisphere, the sun rises to its highest point in the northern part of the sky on the *summer solstice*, June 20, the first day of summer. It slowly moves southward and the days get shorter until three months later when the day and night are equal; this is called the *fall equinox*, September 20, the first day of fall. The sun continues to rise lower in the southern part of the sky, creating cooler temperatures and shorter days. Three months later, the sun rises at its lowest point in the southern sky; this is called *winter solstice*, December 20, the first day of winter. The sun begins to rise higher again, making longer days and moving north until, three months later, the days and nights are equal again; this is called the *spring equinox*, March 20, the first day of spring. The sun continues to rise higher, making longer and warmer days, until it rises to its most northern path again on June 20, the summer solstice. This consistent pattern allowed ancient traditions to plan their livelihood and create the earliest calendars.

Venus

DIAMETER
7,521 miles (slightly smaller than Earth)

LENGTH OF DAY (one full rotation)
243 Earth days

LENGTH OF YEAR (one orbit around sun)
225 Earth days

AVERAGE TEMPERATURE
850° F

HISTORICAL NOTES
William Herschel (1788-1822)

Herschel started making telescopes as a hobby and built over 400 in his lifetime, the largest of which was 40-feet long, half the length of a swimming pool. As his telescopes improved, so did his observations. He was the first person to discover the distant planet of Uranus and its two moons, the two moons of Saturn and he recorded the largest catalogue of *nebulae* up to that time (many of which are now recognized as distant galaxies). He observed that binary stars orbit each other, proving that Newton's laws of gravity hold true outside of our solar system. Because of his discoveries, two of the largest stars in the universe are named after him (including Herschel's Garnet Star or Erakis, p. 32).

SISTER PLANET Venus is sometimes called Earth's "sister planet" because they are similar in size; its diameter is only about 400 miles smaller than that of the earth. However, its size is the only similarity. Its surface temperature is nearly 900 degrees, much hotter than any other planet and it is constantly surrounded by an atmosphere of toxic sulphuric acid. Needless to say, there is no possibility of life existing on our sister planet.

BRIGHTEST PLANET Venus is the brightest object in the sky besides the moon and the sun. Though it is not a large planet, it is relatively close to Earth so the sun's reflection appears quite bright. The brightest star, Sirius, has a magnitude of -2.7 and Venus is a much brighter -4.4 (remember, the lower the number, the brighter the shine).

NAME Because of its stunning brightness, this planet is named after the Roman goddess Venus, comparable to the Greek goddess Athena. It is the only planet named after a woman, perhaps because of its stunning beauty. This brightest "star" in the sky is outstanding at dawn and dusk and has been honored, and even worshipped, in most every past civilization including the Egyptians, Persians, Babylonians, Australian aborigines, North American tribes, ancient China and more.

Viewing Dates of Venus

Sighting Dates	Sighting Time
Nov. 2011 to mid-May 2012	Evening
Late June 2012 to Dec. 2012	Morning
Mid-June 2013 to Dec. 2013	Evening
Feb. 2014 to mid-August 2014	Morning
Late Jan. 2015 to late July 2015	Evening
Late August 2015 to late March 2016	Morning
August 2016 to early March 2017	Evening

STRANGE ROTATION

Earth rotates around its axis every 24 hours. Venus requires 243 earth days to rotate one time around its axis. Now that is one slow moving planet! Besides rotating slowly, it spins in the opposite direction of all the other planets. Astronomers think that a huge rock or other space object might have smashed into Venus millions of years ago, sending it spinning backwards. What a sight that must have been!

Valen Fey
8th grade

ROCK AND GAS

Venus is one of the *terrestrial planets*, but its rocky core is surrounded by a thick gassy cloud. The cloud is mostly Carbon Dioxide, the same stuff that we exhale when we breathe, and Sulfuric Acid, the same stuff that can fry the skin off of a careless chemistry student. This cloud creates a greenhouse effect, in which the sun's rays enter the atmosphere, the heat is trapped beneath the cloud and creates a sizzling hot planet. These hot temperatures and the toxic cloud have fried most technologies that NASA has tried to send to Venus' surface.

MORNING AND EVENING STAR

Venus only appears in the morning and in the evening. For this reason it is often called the *morning star* or the *evening star*, depending on the time of its appearance in the sky. Because its orbit is closer to the sun than the earth's, it always appears near the sun. We see it near the sun in the eastern sky when it rises in the morning and in the western sky after the sun sets, but we never see it in the middle of the night.

Moon

DIAMETER
2,160 miles (1/4 the size of Earth)

ONE ORBIT AROUND EARTH
27 days

TEMPERATURE RANGE
-220° F to 220° F

HISTORICAL NOTES
Edwin Hubble (1889-1953)
Hubble was an American-born astronomer who proved that The Milky Way is not the only galaxy in our universe. In 1922-1923, Hubble worked with the largest telescope in the world at that time, located on Mt. Wilson, in California. Up to that time, astronomers had observed many distant clouds of light and assumed that they were all clouds of gas and newborn stars. Hubble described a new way of measuring distances in space and recognized that these *nebulae* were too far away to be gassy star nurseries. His new understanding and methods led to the discovery of hundreds of galaxies beyond our own, changing the way astronomers viewed the universe.

NO ATMOSPHERE Earth is surrounded by an *atmosphere*, a layer of gases that surround the planet and protect it from intense sun rays, from rocks that are flying through space and it helps to maintain consistent weather. It is like a protective forcefield. In contrast, the moon does not have any atmosphere at all, so it is constantly bombarded by rocks and it has extreme hot and cold temperatures. The craters that are created by the hurling rocks are visible on a full moon night and are quite spectacular when seen through binoculars.

ORIGINS OF THE MOON Why does the moon orbit around Earth? Many scientists believe that a huge rock, perhaps the size of Mars or a bit smaller, smashed into Earth billions of years ago. The impact caused a huge chunk of the earth to break off into space. Over the years, that chunk has rounded off into a ball and is held in orbit by Earth's gravitational pull.

DARK SIDE OF THE MOON The moon does not rotate like the planets do. Earth's gravity has slowed its rotation so that the same side of the moon is always facing towards Earth. Even if you could see the moon every single night of your life, you would always be looking at the exact same features of the moon and will never, ever see the other half of the moon which is always facing out towards space. The half that we do not see is often called the Dark Side of the Moon, as made famous by the band Pink Floyd.

WAXING AND WANING

The moon follows a predictable 28-day cycle. The phases of the moon are determined by how the sun, moon and earth align in the sky. The new moon occurs when the moon is directly between the earth and the sun; the sun's light cannot hit the near-side of the moon, so we cannot see it. A full moon happens when Earth is nearly in between the sun and the moon, when the sun's light hits the moon head on. Following the full moon, it gets incrementally smaller. This is called a *waning moon* and the moon is shaped like a C, as in C-ya-later...it's going away. Following a new moon, the moon gets bigger. This is called a *waxing moon* and it is shaped like a D, as in "how-**dee**"...it is growing and saying hello.

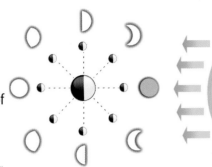

Jaclyn Harris
6th grade

STARGAZING AND THE MOON

Everybody loves a full-moon night. It casts a bluish glow that makes for a bright evening, perfect for playing outside in the moon beams. A full moon can really kill a night of stargazing, though, as the bright light washes out the stars. While a full moon makes for a nice walk in the park, a dark sky is best for seeing

THE MOON AND THE TIDES

While the moon is held in orbit by Earth's gravitational pull, the moon also pulls on Earth, just a little bit. It pulls enough that it affects our oceans. The moon pulls strongest on the side closest to it, so the oceans tend to bulge toward the moon, creating a high-tide. As the moon moves around Earth, the bulge follows it, so the side opposite the moon is drained just a bit, creating a low-tide.

Constellation Difficulty Scale

The constellations in this book are rated to describe how easy or difficult they are to find.

Easy The constellation has several obvious, bright stars; the stars create an obvious pattern and can be seen amidst a bit of light pollution.

Moderate The constellation has at least one obvious, bright star; the stars create an obvious pattern and dark skies are needed to see them.

Difficult There are not obvious, bright stars; the pattern is difficult to identify and dark skies are necessary to see them.

Easy		Moderate		Difficult	
Summer	Bootes	Summer	Aquila	Summer	Hercules
	Summer Triangle		Lyra	Fall	Aries
	Cygnus		Delphinus		
Fall	Pegasus		Corona Borealis	Spring	Coma Berenice
			Sagittarius		Virgo
Winter	Orion		Scorpius	Year-Round	Draco
	Auriga	Fall	Perseus		Cepheus
Year-Round	Big Dipper	Winter	Taurus		Ursa Major
	Cassiopeia		Gemini		Ursa Minor
		Spring	Corvus		
			Leo		

What Else Is Out There?

The night sky is vast. It is much bigger than we can imagine and it is filled with much more than stars, galaxies and nebulae. Following are a few other sky objects previously not mentioned in this book.

SATELLITES While most sky viewing focuses on natural objects, over 10,000 man-made satellites are currently orbiting Earth. Of these, only a hundred or so are large enough to be seen with the naked eye. The brightest satellite is the International Space Station, which orbits Earth at an altitude of 240 miles. Satellites do not create their own light; instead, we see the sun reflecting off of their surface.

SHOOTING STARS Shooting stars are rocks that are flying through space. As they enter the earth's atmosphere, the melting rocks sail through the sky casting a glowing flash of light. The rocks (or *meteoroids*) range in size from pebbles to large boulders. As they catch fire, the "shooting star" is called a *meteor*. Any meteors that don't burn up entirely in the atmosphere land on Earth and are called *meteorites*.

ASTEROIDS Asteroids are rocks that orbit the sun. They range in size from small pebbles to house-sized rocks. They are not visible because they do not create light. Occasionally, some of these asteroids approach pretty close to our own atmosphere. As they fly through space, asteroids break into smaller rocks, some of which fly out of their orbit, burning up in our atmosphere as meteors.

COMETS Comets are similar to asteroids, except instead of rock and metal, they are made mostly of ice and dust. As they approach the sun, they begin to vaporize leaving a long bright tail in their path.

family field guide

Astronomy Timeline

119 BC	Hipparchus catalogues the stars and records planets' orbits in Ancient Greece.
150 AD	Claudius Ptolemy records 48 star constellations in Egypt.
1543	Nicolaus Copernicus publishes the *heliocentric model*, suggesting that the earth and planets revolve around the sun.
1610	Galileo develops the telescope as a useful tool. His observations lead him to agree that the sun is the center of the solar system.
1768	Isaac Newton advances the telescope with his reflective lenses. He proves mathematically that the sun is the center of the solar system.
1800-1817	Charles Messier searches the sky for comets and records over 110 different galaxies, nebulae, star clusters and more.
1810-1822	Willam Herschel improves the telescope and discovers Uranus and other sky features.
1922	Edwin Hubble proves that there are galaxies beyond the Milky Way.
1930	The International Astronomical Union officially records 88 official star constellations.

Map of Astronomy

Bighorn Medicine Wheel (p. 68)

Stonehenge (p. 70)

Greece (p. 26)

Pawnee Tribe (p. 50)

Babylon (p. 20)

China (p. 18)

Anasazi (p. 46)

Arabic Language (p. 64)

Mayans (p. 36)

Incas (p. 54)

Ancient Egypt (p. 44)

Australian Aborigines (p. 38)

family field guide

Spring Star Map

This star map shows the night sky in **March** from 40° North Latitude. The constellations shift westward in the following months; constellations near the western horizon of this map will set and those on the eastern half of the Winter Star Map will rise in **April** and **May**.

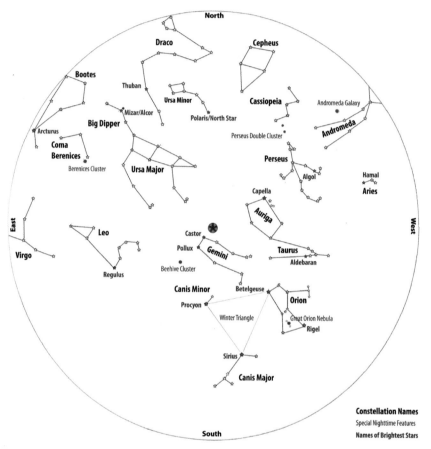

Use the checklist below to find the spring constellations.

March Constellations		Rising April Constellations	Rising May Constellations
Ursa Major	Orion	Bootes	Cygnus
Ursa Minor	Canis Major	Corona Borealis	Lyra
Cepheus	Canis Minor	Corvus	Hercules
Draco	Gemini	Virgo	Scorpius
Cassiopeia	Auriga		
Virgo	Taurus		
Corvus	Aries		
Coma Berenices	Perseus		* not an official constellation
Leo	Andromeda		

family field guide

Summer Star Map

This star map shows the night sky in **June** from 40° North Latitude. The constellations shift westward in the following months; constellations near the western horizon of this map will set and those on the eastern half of the Spring Star Map will rise in **July** and **August**.

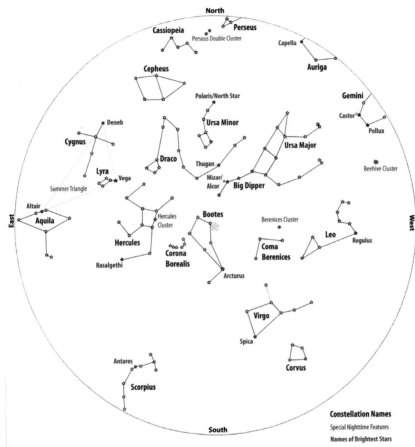

Use the checklist below to find the summer constellations.

Summer Constellations		Rising July Constellations	Rising August Constellations
Ursa Major	Virgo	Pegasus	Perseus
Ursa Minor	Corvus	Andromeda	
Big Dipper*	Corona Borealis	Sagittarius	
Cepheus	Hercules	Delphinus	
Draco	Lyra		
Cassiopeia	Cygnus		
Leo	Auriga		
Coma Berenices	Summer Triangle*		
Bootes	Scorpius		

* not an official constellation

Fall Star Map

This star map shows the night sky in **September** from 40° North Latitude. The constellations shift westward in the following months; constellations near the western horizon of this map will set and those on the eastern half of the Summer Sky Map will rise in **October** and **November**.

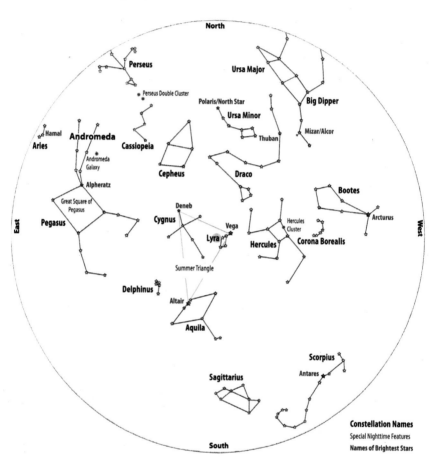

Use the checklist below to find the fall constellations

September Constellations		Rising Oct. Constellations	Rising Nov. Constellations
Andromeda	Draco	Aries	Gemini
Aquila	Hercules	Auriga	Taurus
Aries	Pegasus	Perseus	Orion
Bootes	Perseus		Pleiades Cluster
Big Dipper*	Sagittarius		
Cassiopeia	Scorpius		
Cepheus	Summer Triangle*		
Corona Borealis	Ursa Major		* not an official constellation
Cygnus	Ursa Minor		

family field guide

Winter Star Map

This star map shows the night sky in **December** from 40˚ North Latitude. The constellations shift westward in the following months; constellations near the western horizon of this map will set and those on the eastern half of the Winter Sky Map will rise in **January** and **February**.

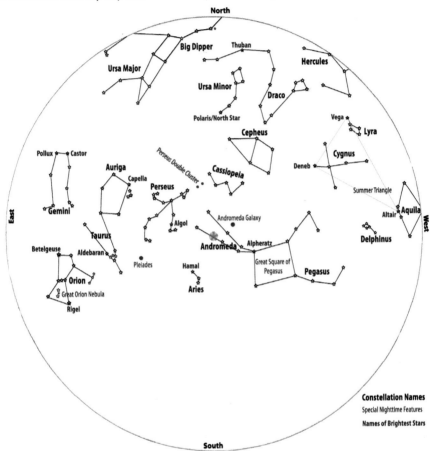

Use the checklist below to find the winter constellations.

Winter Constellations		Rising Jan. Constellations	Rising Feb. Constellations
Ursa Major	Lyra	Canis Major	Leo
Ursa Minor	Cygnus	Canis Minor	
Big Dipper*	Aquila	Winter Triangle*	
Cepheus	Delphinus		
Draco	Aries		
Cassiopeia	Perseus		
Auriga	Taurus		
Andromeda	Orion	* not an official constellation	
Pegasus	Gemini		

Glossary

absolute magnitude Measurement of how bright a star would appear from 32.6 light years away; demonstrates how much light a star emits, not just how bright it appears from Earth.

apparent magnitude Measures the brightness of objects when viewed from Earth.

apparent magnitude scale The measurement scale used to describe apparent magnitude. The original scale measured from 0-6, now it measures a broader range. The lower the number the brighter the light.

astrology The study of the movements and positions of the stars, moon, sun and planets and their supposed influence on human affairs.

astronomy The study of the physical universe beyond the Earth's atmosphere.

asterism A pattern of stars seen in Earth's sky which is not an official constellation.

asteroid Small celestial bodies composed of rock and metal that move around the sun.

atmosphere A layer of gasses surrounding any celestial object, especially planets.

binary star A system of two stars that revolve around each other because of a shared gravitational pull.

double star Also called a "visual double star." A pair of stars that appear very close together, but simply line up in our sightline. The stars are not related and have no gravitational affect on each other.

comet A relatively small, icy mass in the Solar System, usually larger than a meteoroid. When it is close enough to the Sun it displays a visible tail.

constellation A pattern formed by prominent stars with an apparent close proximity to one another.

dwarf planet Any body which is reasonably round, orbits the sun, and has not "cleared its neighborhood" to create its own orbit.

emission nebula A cloud of gas that glows, usually caused by the light of a newborn star or stars within the cloud.

equinox Occurs two times each year when the sun crosses the plane of Earth's equator and day and night are of equal length.

galaxy An enormous system of stars, gases, dust, planets and dark matter that is held together by gravity.

gas giant A large planet that is not mainly composed of rock or other solid matter. Also called Jovian planets. There are four gas giants in our solar system: Jupiter, Saturn, Uranus, and Neptune.

globular cluster A collection of stars that are very tightly bound by gravity giving the cluster a round shape and high density of stars toward the center of the cluster. In contrast, open clusters are held together by a loose gravitational pull and they spread outward over time.

light year (ly) The distance that light travels in 1 year; 5.88 trillion miles. Also a unit of measure to describe the distances of stars and other objects in space.

magnitude The term "magnitude," on its own, usually refers to *apparent magnitude*, the measurement used to describe an object's brightness as viewed from Earth.

Milky Way The galaxy containing Earth and its solar system; consists of millions of stars that can be seen as a hazy band of light stretching across the night sky.

meteor A streak of light in the sky at night that results when a meteoroid hits the earth's atmosphere. Air friction causes the meteoroid to melt, vaporize or explode; commonly called a "shooting star."

meteorite A rocky or metallic object that is the remains of a meteoroid that has reached the earth's surface.

meteoroid Small, solid extraterrestrial rocks that hit the earth's atmosphere.

Glossary (continued)

moon The natural satelite that orbits the earth or any other planet. While planets orbit their star, moons orbit the planets.

nebula An enormous cloud of gas in space (plural: *nebulae*).

North Star The name of the star located directly above Earth's northern axis point. Also called Polaris.

nuclear fusion The combining of small atoms to form larger ones, resulting in a huge release of energy; it is the process that makes the sun shine and the hydrogen bomb explode.

open star cluster A group of stars formed from the same gassy cloud, and are still loosely held together by gravity. In contrast, globular clusters are very tightly bound by gravity.

opposition Describes a planet's location when the earth is directly between the planet and the sun.

orbit The path of one celestial body as it revolves around another; a planet's orbit around the sun or the moon's orbit around the earth.

planet An object in space which orbits a star, is big enough to be rounded by its own gravity, but is not big enough to cause nuclear fusion, and has cleared its "neighboring region" to create its own orbit.

planetary nebula An expanding shell of gas ejected by a red giant star late in its life (this glowing, gassy burp has nothing to do with planets).

pole star A visible star that is approximately aligned with the Earth's axis of rotation; all other stars appear to rotate around the pole star. Polaris, the North Star, is currently the pole star of the Northern hemisphere, but the pole star changes over time.

probe A device used to explore, navigate or measure; usually remote controlled.

red giant A large, old, bright star that has a relatively low surface temperature and is much larger than the sun.

reflecting telescope A telescope consisting of one or more large concave mirrors that produces a magnified image; Isaac Newton invented the reflecting telescope in 1668.

revolution Similar to an orbit. Earth's revolution around the sun requires $365^{1}/_{4}$ days, or one year.

rotation A single, complete turn. Earth completes one rotation around its axis every 24 hours, or one day.

solar Relating to the sun as in solar system and solar energy.

solstice Occurs two times each year when the sun is at its greatest distance from the equator. Winter solstice marks the sun's shortest path over earth; summer solstice marks the sun's longest path over the earth.

sun The star that is the source of light and heat for the planets in the solar system.

supernova A star that explodes and becomes extremely bright in the process.

terrestrial planet A planet composed mainly of rock and iron, similar to that of Earth. The four terrestrial planets in our solar system include Mercury, Venus, Earth and Mars.

variable star A star whose apparent brightness as seen from Earth changes over time, either due to changes in the star's actual brightness, or to changes in the amount of light that is blocked from view.

waxing moon The growing phase of the moon between the new and full moon phases.

waning moon The shrinking phase of the moon between full and new moon phases.

white dwarf A dying star of small or medium size, more solid and dense, but less bright than the sun.

zodiac The 12 constellations that line the path of the Sun across the sky over the course of the year.

Index

(bold page numbers indicate illustrations)

References

Chen, P.K. *A Constellation Album: Stars and Mythology of the Night Sky*.. Cambridge, MA: Sky and Telescope Media, LLC.

Driscoll, Michael. *A Child's Introduction to The Night Sky*. New York: Black Dog & Leventhal Publishers, Inc., 2004. 93. Print.

Hamilton, Edith. *Mythology: Timeless Tales of Gods and Heroes*. New York: Grand Central Publishing, 1942. 495. Print.

Lynch, Mike. *Colorado Starwatch: The Essential Guide to Our Night Sky*. St. Paul, MN: Voyageur Press.

Ray, H.A. *The Stars: A New Way To See Them*. Boston, MA: Houghton Mifflin Company

Scagel, Robin. *Night Sky Atlas: The Universe Mapped, Explored, and Revealed*. 1st ed. New York: DK Publishing, Inc., 2004.

Helpful Astronomy Websites
www.starmaps.com *Print out your own monthly Sky Maps.*
www.stellarium.org *Downloadable software to view the night sky.*

family field guide
— SERIES —

field notes